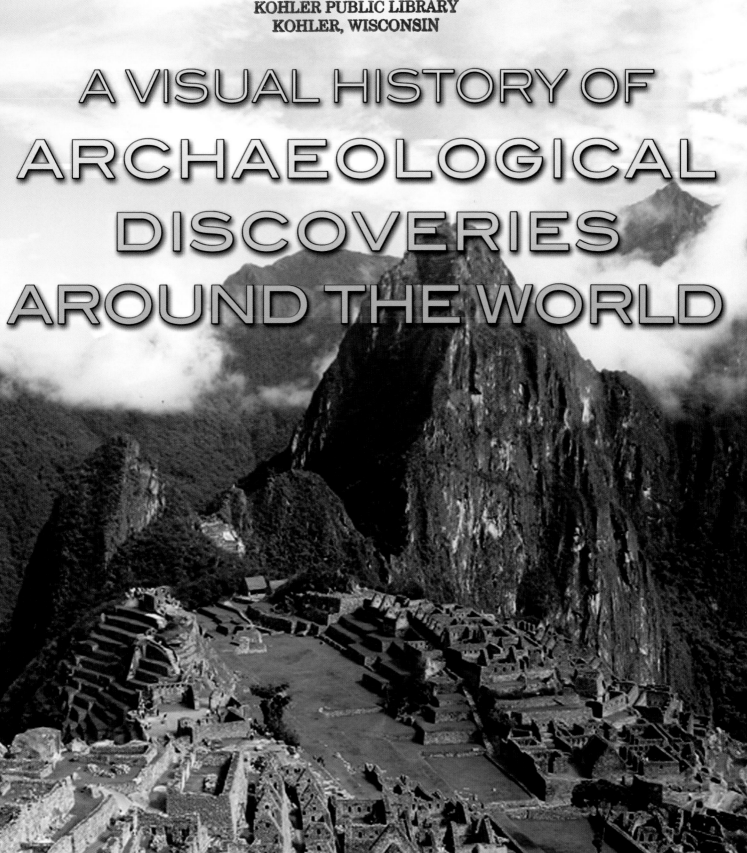

A VISUAL HISTORY OF ARCHAEOLOGICAL DISCOVERIES AROUND THE WORLD

ROSEN PUBLISHING

JOAN SORIANO CAMPOS

This edition published in 2017 by
The Rosen Publishing Group, Inc.
29 East 21st Street
New York, NY 10010

Library of Congress Cataloging-in-Publication Data

Names: Soriano Campos, Joan.
Title: A visual history of archaeological discoveries around the world / Joan Soriano Campos.
Description: New York : Rosen Publishing, 2017. | Series: A visual history of the world | Audience: Grades 7 to 12. | Includes bibliographical references and index.
Identifiers: LCCN 2016035109 | ISBN 9781499465761 (library bound)
Subjects: LCSH: Excavations (Archaeology—Juvenile literature. | Antiquities—Juvenile literature. | Archaeology— Juvenile literature.
Classification: LCC CC171 .S67 2017 | DDC 930.1—dc23
LC record available at https://lccn.loc.gov/2016035109

Manufactured in Malaysia

Metric Conversion Chart

1 inch = 2.54 centimeters; 25.4 millimeters	1 cup = 250 milliliters
1 foot = 30.48 centimeters	1 ounce = 28 grams
1 yard = .914 meters	1 fluid ounce = 30 milliliters
1 square foot = .093 square meters	1 teaspoon = 5 milliliters
1 square mile = 2.59 square kilometers	1 tablespoon = 15 milliliters
1 ton = .907 metric tons	1 quart = .946 liters
1 pound = 454 grams	355 degrees F = 180 degrees Celsius
1 mile = 1.609 kilometers	

Original Idea Nuria Cicero
Editorial Coordination Alberto Hernández
Editorial Team Alberto Moreno de la Fuente, Luciana Rosende, Virginia Iris Fernández, Pablo Pineau, Matías Loewy, Joan Soriano, Mar Valls, Leandro Jema
Proofreaders Marta Kordon, Edgardo D'Elio
Design María Eugenia Hiriart
Layout Laura Ocampo, Clara Miralles, Paola Fornasaro

Photography Age Fotostock, Getty Images, Science Photo Library, National Geographic, Latinstock, Album, ACI, Cordon Press
Illustrations and Infographics Trexel Animation, Trebol Animation, WOW Studio, Sebastián Giacobino, Néstor Taylor, Nuts Studio, Steady in Lab, 3DN, Federico Combi, Pablo Aschei, Leonardo César, 4D News, Rise Studio, Ariel Roldán, Dorian Vandegrift, Zoom Desarrollo Digitales, Marcelo Regalado.

Contents

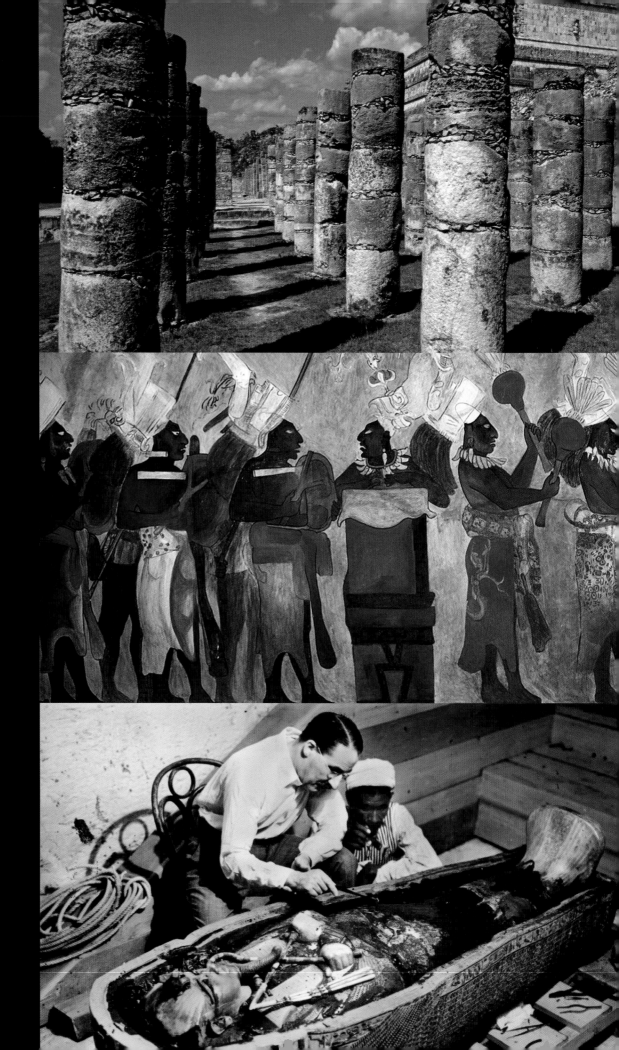

Introduction

The past continues to live on in the present. The remains of the men and women who lived hundreds of thousands of years ago, the traces of hominoids who populated the **Earth** millions of years ago ... these things allow us to discover the past in always greater detail thanks to advances in **technology**. The application of radiocarbon dating and the development of DNA analysis, both beginning in the second half of the twentieth century, have allowed the science of archaeology, in its never-ending quest to unravel our distant past, to take giant steps forward.

Although **humans** have always had a desire to find out about our ancestors and their way of life, it was not until two centuries ago that this heritage began to be studied in detail. What originally motivated archaeological searches in many cases was the interest in locating objects of **value**, until laws protecting cultural heritage were introduced so as to end these practices, carried out routinely by governments and private collectors alike.

Thus, interest in the past from a strictly scientific point of view is relatively recent. Archaeology was considered a branch of **history** until, at the end of the nineteenth century, it achieved categorization as an academic discipline and began to incorporate **scientific** methodology. Without this transformation, we would not have been able to study, with even minimal scientific rigor, the Prehistoric times, the history of cultures lacking written sources, or cultures that simply did not use writing.

The discipline of Archaeology has been a determining factor in understanding key events in the history of Mankind. The findings, when organized chronologically, continually rewrite our history with increasing detail. Some discoveries, especially material remains from thousands of years ago, have destroyed **hypotheses** that were upheld for centuries and everything resting on them in an instant, as if they were a house of cards. Then that unexpected, amazing, most recent discovery develops a new narrative of the past, a new understanding of the history of Mankind.

Chronology

1879
▶ **ALTAMIRA**
Rock paintings are discovered in the caves of Altamira (Spain). These feature the zenith of Paleolithic cave art in Europe.

1901
▶ **EXCAVATION OF THE VALLEY OF THE KINGS**
Theodore M. Davis begins excavation in the Valley of the Kings (Egypt). He finds 30 tombs over the next 12 years.

1854
▶ **THE FINDING OF UR**
John George Taylor, British consul in Mesopotamia, identifies and initiates the excavation of the ruins of the ancient Sumerian city of Ur, forgotten for more than 2000 years.

1763
▶ **POMPEII**
Identification of the ruins of the Roman city of Pompeii (Italy), buried in 79 AD by the volcanic eruption of Mount Vesuvius.

1822
▶ **HIEROGLYPHICS**
Jean-François Champollion announces the first deciphering of royal names in hieroglyphic writing, with the help of the Rosetta Stone.

1871
▶ **TROY**
German archaeologist Heinrich Schliemann discovers the remains of legendary Troy, central to Homer's *Iliad*. His finding seems to confirm the existence of the metropolis, though some archaeologists doubt that it is truly Troy.

1974

▶ **THE TERRACOTTA WARRIORS**
Fortuitous discovery of the Terracotta Army of Qin Shi Huangdi, near Xi'an (China).

1978

▶ **LAETOLI**
Mary Leakey discovers the oldest known hominoid footprints in Laetoli (Tanzania).

1926

▶ **NAZCA LINES**
Julio César Tello, Toribio Mejía, and Alfred L. Kroeber discover, when climbing a nearby hill, the immense drawings engraved by the Nazca culture in the ground of the Ica region (Peru). They are only visible from a notable height or from the air.

1911

▶ **MACHU PICCHU**
The "lost" Inca city is located by the U.S. explorer Hiram Bingham.

1922

▶ **TUTANKHAMEN**
Howard Carter discovers the young Egyptian pharaoh's tomb, the first and only practically intact find in Egypt.

1949

▶ **CARBON-14**
American Willard Frank Libby develops radiocarbon dating, which proves pivotal in the advance of archaeology.

1958

▶ **ÇATALHÖYÜK**
Its discovery revealed the existence of a prominent center of advanced Neolithic culture in Anatolia (Turkey).

1987

▶ **LORD OF SIPÁN**
Peruvian Walter Alva finds the tomb of the Lord of Sipán, the most lavish tomb in the Americas, in a Moche ceremonial center in Peru.

1994

▶ **CARAL**
Ruth Shady discovers the highly valuable archaeological remains of the city of Caral (Peru), the oldest in the Americas, first discovered in 1905.

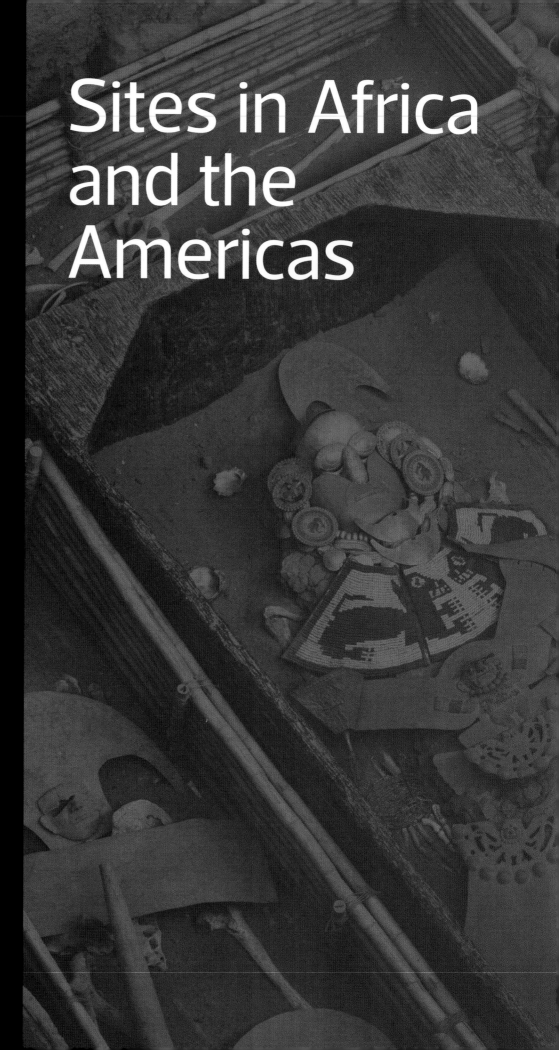

Sites in Africa and the Americas

Chapter 1

The first hominoid footprints we have evidence of date to some 3.6 million years ago. They were discovered by Mary Leakey in 1978 in Laetoli, Tanzania. By 1959, Louis and Mary Leakey had discovered the remains of hominoids in Olduvai, also in Tanzania, confirming the Darwinian theory regarding the African origin of humankind. It was the science of archaeology that demonstrated to the world that Africa was the birthplace of humankind. On the same continent, the ancient Egyptians erected monumental structures and bequeathed a cultural and artistic heritage so extraordinary that their civilization merited a specialized line of study: Egyptology. Few archaeologists would disagree that the finding of Tutankhamen's tomb was the most outstanding find in the history of archaeology.

A world away from the impressive Egyptian temples and tombs, Pre-Columbian civilizations in the Americas developed a cultural heritage of enormous value, first in Mesoamerica and later in the Central Andes. Entire cities such as Chichen Itza, Teotihuacan, and Machu Picchu; splendid tombs such as that of the Lord of Sipán; and sophisticated systems of governmental organization such as that of the Inca; these clearly show the contribution of the Americas to mankind's history.

The Laetoli Footprints

In the late 1970s, British archaeologist Mary Leakey and her team discovered the oldest known footprints belonging to a direct ancestor of humankind, *Australopithecus afarensis*, at the Laetoli site (Tanzania).

The First Bipeds

Although there are various theories, the most widespread is that the group of footprints found in Laetoli, some 3.6 million years old, correspond to three bipedal individuals: a pair of adult hominoids between 1.2 and 1.5 m all, and a child who probably followed them, stepping in their tracks. The finding consists of two lines of footprints running for some 30 m, from south to north. The Tanzanian government is working to move the remains, damaged by tree roots and water drainage, to a museum.

VOLCANIC ASH
Ash from the Sadiman volcano some 20 km from the site, combined with light rain, created a smooth surface similar to cement, which the hominoids stepped in.

Almost Human Footprints

Several studies have verified that the Laetoli footprints correspond to bipedal individuals who walked erect, and in fact they are very similar to those of a human being. The big toe is not separated from the others, as is the case with simians, and a cast of the footprint reveals the typical lengthwise human arch on the sole.

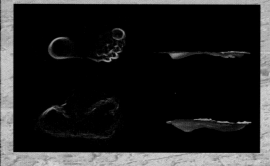

IN 3D
These 3D images by professor David Raichlen (University of Arizona) show the similarity between a current human footprint (above) and a Laetoli footprint (below).

NO HURRY
Analysis of the footprints determined that the three individuals, likely a family, were not fleeing a volcanic eruption, but were walking peacefully.

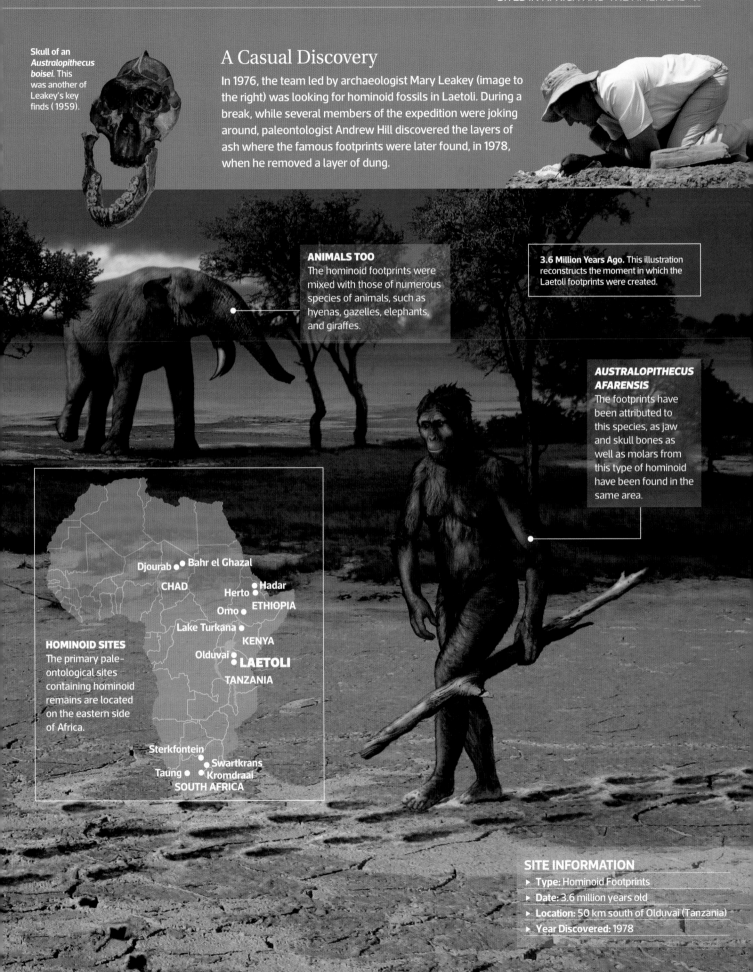

Skull of an *Australopithecus boisei*. This was another of Leakey's key finds (1959).

A Casual Discovery

In 1976, the team led by archaeologist Mary Leakey (image to the right) was looking for hominoid fossils in Laetoli. During a break, while several members of the expedition were joking around, paleontologist Andrew Hill discovered the layers of ash where the famous footprints were later found, in 1978, when he removed a layer of dung.

ANIMALS TOO
The hominoid footprints were mixed with those of numerous species of animals, such as hyenas, gazelles, elephants, and giraffes.

3.6 Million Years Ago. This illustration reconstructs the moment in which the Laetoli footprints were created.

AUSTRALOPITHECUS AFARENSIS
The footprints have been attributed to this species, as jaw and skull bones as well as molars from this type of hominoid have been found in the same area.

HOMINOID SITES
The primary paleontological sites containing hominoid remains are located on the eastern side of Africa.

Djourab • • Bahr el Ghazal
CHAD
Herto • • Hadar
Omo • **ETHIOPIA**
Lake Turkana •
KENYA
Olduvai • • **LAETOLI**
TANZANIA

Sterkfontein •
• Swartkrans
Taung • • Kromdraai
SOUTH AFRICA

SITE INFORMATION
▸ **Type:** Hominoid Footprints
▸ **Date:** 3.6 million years old
▸ **Location:** 50 km south of Olduvai (Tanzania)
▸ **Year Discovered:** 1978

The Pyramids of Giza

The necropolis of Giza is located on a large plateau near Cairo. Its three major pyramids, funerary monuments created to worship the pharaohs, are the grandest architectural expression of the Ancient Egyptian Empire.

Great Western
Cemetery
(Mastabas)

Khufu's
Pyramid

Khafra's
Pyramid

Subsidiary Pyramid

Perimeter Walls

Menkaure's
Pyramid

Pyramids of
Menkaure's Queens

Menkaure's
Funerary Temples

Giants on the Plain

While Egypt has at least 120 pyramids, the Giza pyramids are without a doubt the most famous, due to their height as well as the quality of workmanship.

SITE INFORMATION
▶ **Type:** Necropolis
▶ **Date:** 2575 BC to 2134 BC
▶ **Location:** 20 km from Cairo (Egypt)
▶ **Area:** 160 km²

Chronology of the Construction of the Major Pyramids

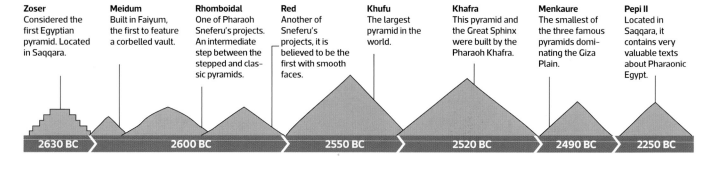

Zoser
Considered the first Egyptian pyramid. Located in Saqqara.

Meidum
Built in Faiyum, the first to feature a corbelled vault.

Rhomboidal
One of Pharaoh Sneferu's projects. An intermediate step between the stepped and classic pyramids.

Red
Another of Sneferu's projects, it is believed to be the first with smooth faces.

Khufu
The largest pyramid in the world.

Khafra
This pyramid and the Great Sphinx were built by the Pharaoh Khafra.

Menkaure
The smallest of the three famous pyramids dominating the Giza Plain.

Pepi II
Located in Saqqara, it contains very valuable texts about Pharaonic Egypt.

| 2630 BC | 2600 BC | 2550 BC | 2520 BC | 2490 BC | 2250 BC |

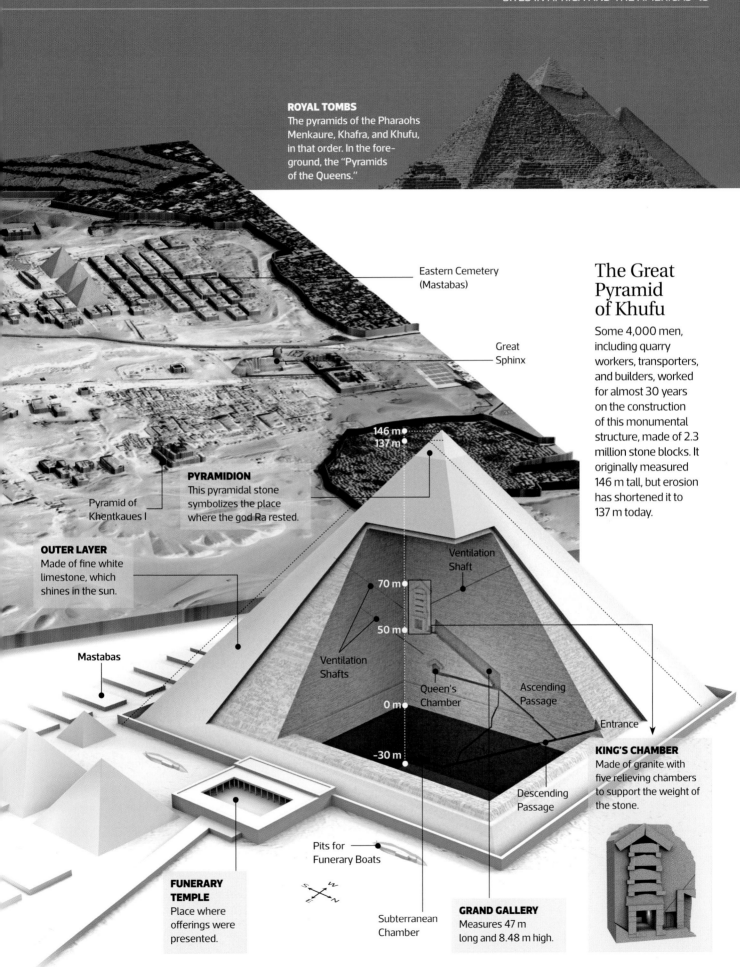

ROYAL TOMBS
The pyramids of the Pharaohs Menkaure, Khafra, and Khufu, in that order. In the foreground, the "Pyramids of the Queens."

Eastern Cemetery (Mastabas)

Great Sphinx

The Great Pyramid of Khufu

Some 4,000 men, including quarry workers, transporters, and builders, worked for almost 30 years on the construction of this monumental structure, made of 2.3 million stone blocks. It originally measured 146 m tall, but erosion has shortened it to 137 m today.

PYRAMIDION
This pyramidal stone symbolizes the place where the god Ra rested.

Pyramid of Khentkaues I

146 m
137 m

OUTER LAYER
Made of fine white limestone, which shines in the sun.

Ventilation Shaft

70 m

50 m

Ventilation Shafts

Queen's Chamber

Ascending Passage

Mastabas

0 m

Entrance

-30 m

KING'S CHAMBER
Made of granite with five relieving chambers to support the weight of the stone.

Descending Passage

FUNERARY TEMPLE
Place where offerings were presented.

Pits for Funerary Boats

Subterranean Chamber

GRAND GALLERY
Measures 47 m long and 8.48 m high.

The Rosetta Stone

The writing system used in Ancient Egypt from 3100 BC to 400 AD was not deciphered until 1822. The finding of the Rosetta Stone enabled the meaning of the hieroglyphs to be revealed.

Three Types of Writing

The Rosetta stone is a black granite stone engraved with three distinct forms of writing: Ancient Egyptian hieroglyphic, Demotic, and Ancient Greek. It was discovered on July 15, 1799, by soldiers in Napoleon's army near the city of el-Rashid (Rosetta). Since 1802, it has resided in the British Museum.

DECREE OF PHARAOH PTOLEMY V
The text found on the stone corresponds to a decree issued by a council of priests ratifying the royal cult of Ptolemy V, then 13 years of age, on the first anniversary of his coronation. It was published in Memphis, Egypt, in 196 BC.

SITE INFORMATION
- **Type:** Engraved Stone
- **Date:** 196 AD
- **Location:** El-Rashid, 65 km east of Alexandria (Egypt)
- **Year Discovered:** 1799

Text in Hieroglyphics (Writing of the gods)

Expanded Text

Text in Demotic (Writing of the people)

114 cm

Text in Ancient Greek (Writing of the government)

72 cm

27 cm

The System of Hieroglyphic Writing

It is mixed: ideographic and consonantal. Thus, it is made up of:

IDEOGRAMS
Signs that represent objects exclusively in graphic form.

⊙ → r' → Ra = Day/Sun

PHONOGRAMS
Signs that represent the pronunciation of a letter.

→ y

SYLLABIC
Signs that represent the pronunciation of more than one consonant.

→ **nb** → neb
→ **iwn** → iun
→ **rnpt** → renepet

DETERMINATIVE
Signs that act as markers in words to indicate their semantic function.

△ → Advance
△ → Retreat

The Hieroglyphic Alphabet

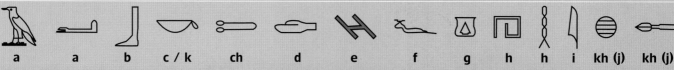

| a | a | b | c / k | ch | d | e | f | g | h | h | i | kh (j) | kh (j) |

THOMAS YOUNG
Demonstrated that the hieroglyphs on the Rosetta Stone corresponded to the sounds of a real name, that of Ptolemy.

Definitive Deciphering

French Egyptologist Jean–François Champollion (1790–1832) was the first to decipher the complete text of the Rosetta Stone and the sounds that corresponded to each of the Egyptian hieroglyphs.

Groups of Symbols

Hieroglyphs were not written in linear sequence, like the letters of an alphabet system. They were grouped in imaginary squares or rectangles for a harmonious arrangement.

READING DIRECTION

The Egyptians wrote both left to right and right to left. Thomas Young was the first to discover that hieroglyphic reading direction was determined by the orientation of the heads of figures such as animals.

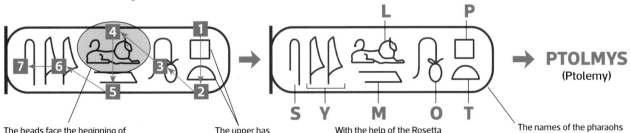

PTOLMYS
(Ptolemy)

The heads face the beginning of the words and indicate the reading direction.

The upper has priority over the lower.

With the help of the Rosetta Stone, sounds were assigned to the symbols.

The names of the pharaohs or queens were enclosed in cartouches like these.

j　　l　　m　　m　　n　　o　　p　　q　　r　　s/z　s　　t　　u(w)　w　　y　　y

The Valley of the Kings

For 500 years, the Valley of the Kings was the preferred burial site of the pharaohs of the New Kingdom of Ancient Egypt. From the first excavations in the nineteenth century until now, a total of 65 tombs and burial chambers have been found in this necropolis.

New Customs

During the New Kingdom (1539 to 1075 BC), the pharaohs switched from pyramids—which were very costly and subject to looting—to subterranean tombs. They also placed them in a funerary site that was difficult to access: the Valley of the Kings. This necropolis houses the celebrated tombs of Tutankhamen and Ramesses II, as well as many other pharaohs and royal persons from the Eighteenth, Nineteenth, and Twentieth Dynasties.

Tomb Entrance

Discreet access to the tombs hid great riches, preserved at the end of long galleries that sometimes reached lengths of 100 m or more.

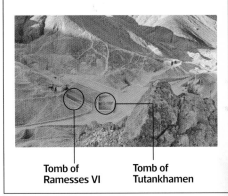

Tomb of Ramesses VI

Tomb of Tutankhamen

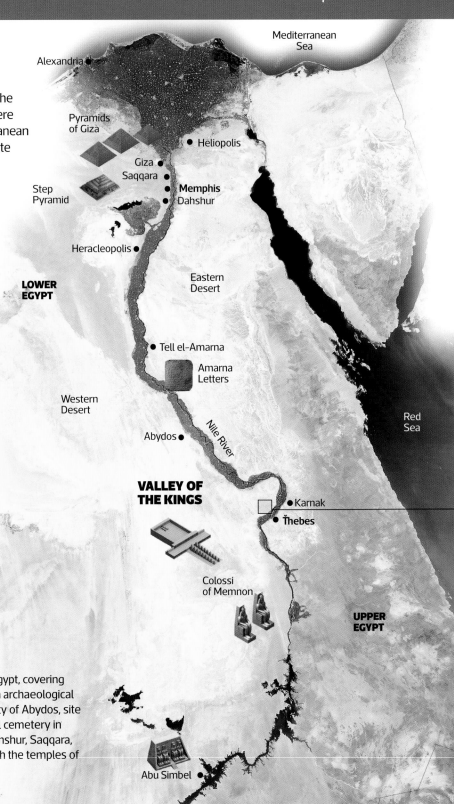

Mediterranean Sea

Alexandria

Pyramids of Giza

Heliopolis

Giza

Saqqara

Step Pyramid

Memphis
Dahshur

Heracleopolis

LOWER EGYPT

Eastern Desert

Tell el-Amarna

Amarna Letters

Western Desert

Nile River

Abydos

VALLEY OF THE KINGS

Karnak

Thebes

Red Sea

Colossi of Memnon

UPPER EGYPT

Abu Simbel

Legacy of Ancient Egypt

The Nile Valley is filled with ruins from Ancient Egypt, covering three thousand years of history. The best-known archaeological sites in order of antiquity are: the pre-dynastic city of Abydos, site of the Great Temple of Osiris and the oldest royal cemetery in the world; Memphis, with the necropolises of Dahshur, Saqqara, and Giza, which house the pyramids; Thebes, with the temples of Karnak and Luxor and the Valley of the Kings.

Looting of the Treasures

Despite the fact that the entrances were hidden, almost all of the tombs discovered in the Valley of the Kings had been looted before the Twentieth Dynasty ended its reign. Tutankhamen's tomb was the first found practically intact, even though it had not been spared visits by thieves.

ROYAL FAN
Among the valuable treasures preserved in Tutankhamen's tomb is this fan covered in gold.

Two Valleys in One

The Valley of the Kings is actually two valleys: the East Valley (see illustration), which houses the majority of the tombs, catalogued with the initials KV (Kings' Valley); and the West Valley, also known as the Valley of the Monkeys, in which four tombs are found, catalogued as WV (West Valley).

Thutmose III **5**
Seti II
Thutmose I **3**
Siptah
Thutmose IV
Amenhotep II
Horemheb
Hatshepsut **4**
Ramesses X   Seti I
Ramesses III
Ramesses I
Ramesses VI
Mernetpah
Tutankhamen **1**
2
Ramesses IX   Ramesses II

Valle de los Reyes.
Principales tumbas reales del valle oriental.

Tentkaru
Userhet

Ramesses XI
Yuya and Tjuyu
Ramesses IV

Expanded Area

SITE INFORMATION

Type: Necropolis	
Date: approx. 1500 BC	
Location: Near Luxor (Egypt), on the western bank of the Nile	
Year Discovered: 1708	

1 **TUTANKHAMEN**
(1332-1323 BC)
18th Dynasty. Son of Akhenaten, he restored the worship of Amun. He is the best-known pharaoh due to the discovery of his nearly intact tomb in 1922.

2 **RAMESSES II**
(1290-1224 BC)
19th Dynasty. Pharaoh, warrior, and builder. He led the famous battle of Qadesh against the Hittite Empire. He also built the Abu Simel and Ramesseum temples.

3 **THUTMOSE I**
(1504-1492 BC)
18th Dynasty. Extended the kingdom to Upper Nubia and waged war on the banks of the Euphrates. Founder of the Theban necropolis in the Valley of the Kings.

4 **HATSHEPSUT**
(1479-1457 BC)
18th Dynasty. Heiress of Thutmose I, she was the most powerful Egyptian queen-pharaoh. Ordered the building of the Djeser-Djeseru temple.

5 **THUTMOSE III**
(1457-1425 BC)
18th Dynasty. Provided the Egyptian Empire with its largest expansion. Subjugated Middle Eastern and Eastern Mediterranean kingdoms. Built Karnak temple.

The Tomb of Tutankhamen

This goldmine of archaeology, discovered in 1922, follows the same structure as the rest of the tombs in the Valley of the Kings: a corridor leads to an antechamber which then leads to the burial chamber.

The Lost Tomb

Only luck kept the tomb of Tutankhamen nearly intact. Two centuries after it was built, the Egyptians carved the tomb of Pharaoh Ramesses VI nearly directly on top of it. The work led to the tomb of Tutankhamen being covered by rocks.

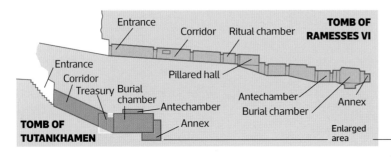

TOMB OF RAMESSES VI

Entrance
Corridor   Ritual chamber
Pillared hall
Antechamber
Burial chamber
Annex
Enlarged area

TOMB OF TUTANKHAMEN

Entrance
Corridor
Treasury   Burial chamber
Antechamber
Annex

SITE INFORMATION

- ▸ **Type:** Tomb
- ▸ **Date:** 1327 BC
- ▸ **Location:** Valley of the Kings, Luxor (Egypt)
- ▸ **Year Discovered:** 1922

1,7 m

2 m

ANNEX
Another entrance to an adjoining room was hidden behind the furniture. It was the last to be examined. It contained a wide variety of piled-up stones.

THE CORRIDOR
It was covered—as were the stairs—with stone rubble.

ANTECHAMBER
Sealed by walls and full of the Pharaoh's personal objects, the majority of which were made of gold or gilded wood.

The Treasury

The "Treasury" is behind an open door of the burial chamber. A statue of Anubis stands guard over the entrance and the Canopic Shrine, protected by four goddesses.

The Canopic Shrine
It contains the organs of the Pharaoh: the liver, lungs, stomach, and intestines were removed from his body to preserve them.

Egyptian goddess

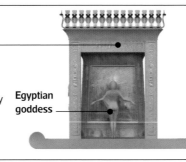

Gold chest
It contained four cases or "jars."

Case   Organs

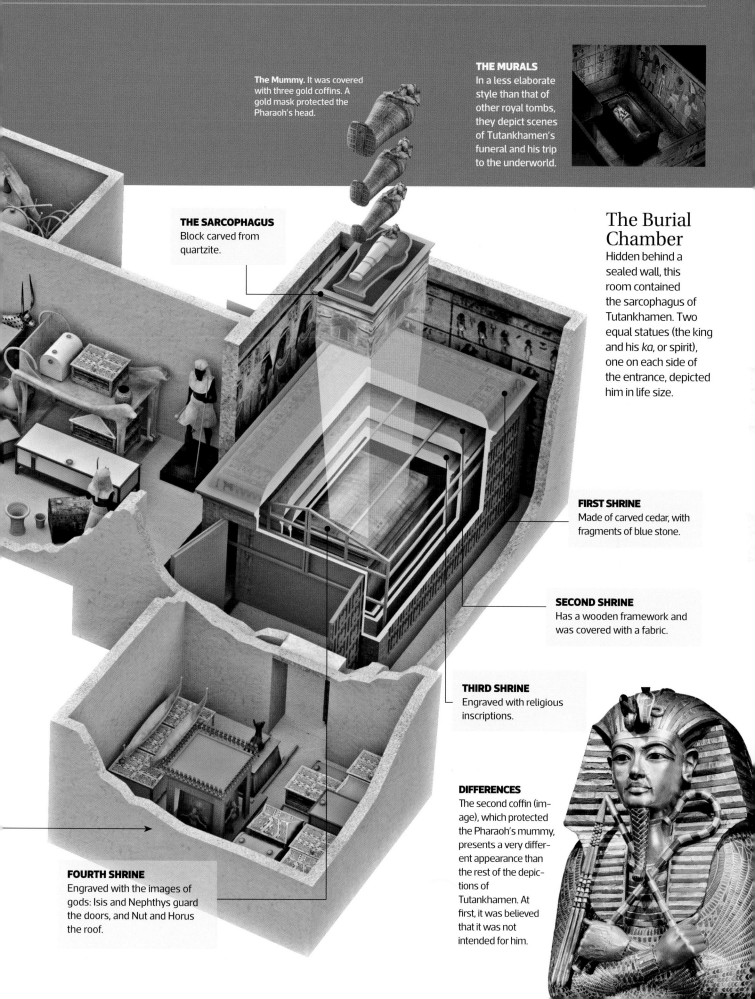

The Mummy. It was covered with three gold coffins. A gold mask protected the Pharaoh's head.

THE MURALS
In a less elaborate style than that of other royal tombs, they depict scenes of Tutankhamen's funeral and his trip to the underworld.

THE SARCOPHAGUS
Block carved from quartzite.

The Burial Chamber

Hidden behind a sealed wall, this room contained the sarcophagus of Tutankhamen. Two equal statues (the king and his *ka*, or spirit), one on each side of the entrance, depicted him in life size.

FIRST SHRINE
Made of carved cedar, with fragments of blue stone.

SECOND SHRINE
Has a wooden framework and was covered with a fabric.

THIRD SHRINE
Engraved with religious inscriptions.

DIFFERENCES
The second coffin (image), which protected the Pharaoh's mummy, presents a very different appearance than the rest of the depictions of Tutankhamen. At first, it was believed that it was not intended for him.

FOURTH SHRINE
Engraved with the images of gods: Isis and Nephthys guard the doors, and Nut and Horus the roof.

The Sacred City of Caral

Considered the oldest city in the Americas, Caral was built five thousand years ago, during the American Pre-Ceramic Period. It was the center of the Norte Chico civilization, one of the first complex societies developed in the north-central area of Peru.

Ancient Urban Center

Named Caral-Supe because of its location in the Supe River valley. It is estimated that it came to have around 3,000 inhabitants, and that it had a wide variety of buildings: temples, housing, amphitheater, warehouses, altars, etc. Its temple, known as the Greater Pyramid, is outstanding.

The Main Pyramid

This great building served as an administrative as well as religious center, and it dominated the life of the entire city due to its great size. As an architectural complex, its main components were the circular sunken plaza and the pyramid with stepped platforms around it. All the outer walls were made of stone. It measured 149 m long by 170 m wide. Its height reached 29 m in the north sector.

WEST WING
Included a complex of large terraces accessed by a side staircase.

ATRIUM
This was an impressive ceremonial space, with a central fire pit and stepped walkways.

CENTRAL STAIRCASE
The main entrance to the ceremonial facilities.

CIRCULAR PLAZA
Accessed by two large staircases, it was a space for the bartering of products such as squash, beans, and chili peppers.

TERRACES
The terraces were overlaid on one another, and were a place for people to come together to carry out their tasks.

Ancient Civilization

Studies using Carbon-14 dating have determined that this civilization is 5,000 years old, compared to which Harappa in India, Sumeria in Mesopotamia, China, and Egypt are considered modern.

ICON OF CARAL
One of the figures made of raw clay found at the Huanca Pyramid in Caral. Represents an individual with high social status.

HALL
Ceremonial rites were practiced in this and other rooms. It was adorned with alcoves.

ALTAR
It had an underground ventilation duct.

SITE INFORMATION

Type: City
Date: 3000 BC
Location: Supe Valley, 200 km north of Lima (Peru)
Year Discovered: 1994

FIRE PIT
The Altar of Sacred Fire was located in a room decorated with friezes and alcoves. Offerings were burned there as a means of communicating with the gods.

Map of Caral-Supe

Made up of several structures, it occupies an area of 65 hectares. The most notable findings include 32 buildings—six of which are pyramid-shaped, and traces of several fire pits used for ritual offerings (the main compounds below). Instruments made of bone, wood, and stone –such as trumpets and flutes– were found among the ruins.

N

1 Greater Pyramid		**5** Huanca Pyramid	
2 Lesser Pyramid		**6** Gallery Pyramid	
3 Quarry Pyramid		**7** Temple of the Circular Altar	
4 Residential Unit		**8** Amphitheater Pyramid	

EAST WING
Wing with more overlaid terraces, seven in total, with rooms and staircases connecting them.

Chavín de Huántar

At the center of the Chavín civilization, this Peruvian archaeological site is one of the best-preserved pre-Columbian ceremonial complexes. The sanctuary is composed of the first Old Temple and the New Temple built partially on top of the first.

The New Temple and the Old Temple

Surrounded by impressive walls up to 12 m high, the shrine was richly adorned with naturalistic motifs and anthropomorphic figures engraved or carved in stone. A series of buildings stand out, such as the Circular Plaza and the Lanzón Gallery, which houses the most famous sculpture of the area.

APPROXIMATE MODEL
The recreation of this image is based on the works of Peruvian archaeologist Luis Guillermo Lumbreras, one of the most notable scholars of the Chavín culture.

NEW TEMPLE
It had a doorway with two columns which was accessed by staircases that started directly beside the Mosna River.

ADORNMENT
The walls were decorated with engraved images of birds, snakes, felines, and protruding bald heads.

A Game-Changing Discovery

Chavín de Huántar is located at a key crossroads of the Peruvian plateau, between two rivers, and on the foothills of the Blanca mountain range, in the current province of Huari. In 1919, Julio C. Tello, considered the father of Peruvian archaeology, discovered the Chavín and Paracas cultures, and after sorting the collected evidence, proved their pre-Inca origin.

Raimondi Stela

This famous monolith discovered at Chavín de Huántar is almost 2 m high by 73 cm wide and 17 cm thick. Engraved on only one of its sides, it shows a deity holding two staffs.

CHAVÍN POTTERY

The most characteristic pieces are those with two upper handles and a mouth. To the right, a piece made between 700 and 500 BC.

INTERNAL CANALS

Narrow corridors and underground galleries are all throughout the structure. Many were used as drainage ducts to channel water to the river.

OLD TEMPLE

A great closed structure that houses galleries, ventilation shafts, and drains.

The Lanzón Monolith

Also called the "Great Image," it is the most well-known sculpture from the Chavín culture. Associated with a deity, it represents a supernatural figure with a feline face, fangs, and claws, the eyes of a snake, and snakes for hair.

4.53 m

LANZÓN GALLERY

Erected in the Old Temple, it is a quad-rangular area that contains the famous Chavín sculpture, the Lanzón.

THE ROAR OF THE TEMPLE

Below the platform was a system of canals that carried water from the river. The noise they made was inter-preted as an oracle.

FELINE MOUTH

In a shape similar to that of a spear, the sculp-ture is 4.53 meters high. Large ring-shaped earrings, a beaded necklace, and bracelets are featured among its adornments.

PLAZA

Circular and sunk into the ground, it has a diameter of 21 m. It was decorated with stone friezes with figures of jaguars and anthropo-morphic figures.

SITE INFORMATION

▸ **Type:** Temple
▸ **Date:** 1500 BC (apogee: 500 BC)
▸ **Location:** 462 km to the northeast of Lima (Peru)
▸ **Year Discovered:** 1919
▸ **Altitude:** 3.177 m above sea level

The Nazca Lines

South of Lima (Peru), in a desert area spanning almost 450 km², the Nazca culture left a strange and mysterious legacy carved into the earth: hundreds of geometric lines and shapes, and over 70 artistic representations.

Types of Lines

Within the group of lines and symbols made by the Nazca, a variety of designs can be made out due to their shapes and hypothetical meanings. Usually the lines measure about a yard wide and can be up to several miles long. Some are straight and others are in spiral or zigzag shapes. They can be very clear, or somewhat faded, depending on the period during which they were created.

ENTRANCE AND EXIT
Several of the Nazca designs have an entrance and exit line, which permits covering the circuit without crossing any lines, and reinforces the idea that the drawings were ritual paths.

STRAIGHT LINES
The hills and uneven ground did not prove to be an obstacle for the Nazca people. Significant detours are not perceived.

The spider. This is one of the most well-known figures and is formed by a single continuous line.

ZIGZAG AND SPIRAL LINES
For the first, they marked the spacing of the pattern precisely, like a modulated frequency signal, while the spiral lines could have been drawn using a post with a cord wrapped around it, moving further and further from a central point.

All Kinds of Figures

In addition to thousands of lines, the Nazca plateau is full of designs, both geometric shapes –the most common being trapezoids and rectangles, as well as animals– the monkey, spider, and hummingbird, among others– and human and plant forms.

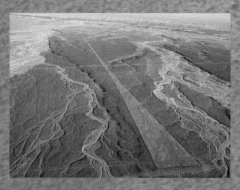

Trapezoids. In this type of shape, the vertex is possibly pointing toward the horizon, perhaps with the intention of pointing out the setting of the sun at specific periods.

SITE INFORMATION
- **Type:** Geoglyphs and lines
- **Date:** 500 BC (to 600 AD)
- **Location:** 450 km (south of Lima (Peru)
- **Year Discovered:** 1926
- **Area:** 450 Km²

Polychrome Pottery. The Nazca people developed an extraordinary ability and creativity in pottery.

Masters of Water

One of the most interesting legacies of the Nazca culture is the magnificent network of drains, aqueducts, canals, and underground galleries they built to carry water to their crops. In the image you see a puquio, the typical Nazca well.

AERIAL OBSERVATION

Researchers such as Joe Nickell of the University of Kentucky reproduced the figures using technology that would have existed at the time, without aerial observation. With careful planning and simple techniques, a small group of people can recreate even the larger figures within a few days.

Symbols and lines are visible

The lines are barely visible, the shapes are not defined

Only the contrast between the rocks and the yellowish ground can be distinguished

SYMMETRY

The mandibles are drawn with particular attention to symmetry that is not present in the majority of the drawings. A long straight line (made later) crosses through the drawing.

THE GROUND

The surface is made up of a layer of pebbles of a dark reddish color, caused by oxidation. Removing the surface stones produces the color contrast of the lines.

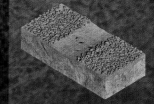

CELESTIAL MAP

German archaeologist Maria Reiche maintained that the Spider was a representation of the constellation of Orion, although the little data that supports this hypothesis is not conclusive.

The Tomb of the Lord of Sipán

In 1987, the most impressive royal tomb discovered thus far in the Americas, that of the Lord of Sipán, was found in the north of Peru, at a large Moche ceremonial complex. It contained very beautiful jewels in several layered tombs.

Moche Royal Burial

This archaeological complex, which was given the name Huaca Rajada, was built by the Moche people, a rich culture that developed on the northern coast of Peru a thousand years before the Inca and flourished between the first and seventh centuries. Within the complex, which has three main tombs, the most outstanding is the spectacular tomb of the Lord of Sipán, buried with eight of his subjects who were probably sacrificed.

Reconstruction. Image of a reproduction of the tomb, displayed at the Museum of Royal Tombs of Sipán.

Layers of Tombs

The Moche sanctuary of Huaca Rajada originally consisted of a stepped adobe pyramid. As the pyramid was restructured for maintenance reasons, new levels were incorporated and new platforms were built on top. Eight architectural construction phases have been detected. The tomb of the Lord of Sipán is found on the first (highest) level, while that of the "Old Lord of Sipán" is on one of the lowest levels.

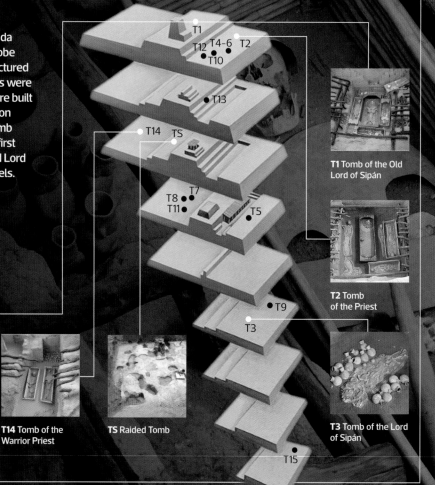

T1
T12 T4-6 T2
T10
T13
T14 TS
T7
T8
T11 T5
T9
T3
T15

T1 Tomb of the Old Lord of Sipán

T2 Tomb of the Priest

T3 Tomb of the Lord of Sipán

Repository of Offerings. Before discovering the tomb of the Lord of Sipán, the archaeologists came across a chamber which held 1,137 pieces of pottery.

T14 Tomb of the Warrior Priest

TS Raided Tomb

Exceptional Artisans

The Moche were great metal smiths. They melted, rolled, forged, embossed and welded copper, gold, and silver. They also came to use techniques such as tumbaga to give the appearance of gold to objects which, in reality, were made mostly of copper. In the image, an original ceremonial diadem.

SITE INFORMATION

▸ **Type:** Tomb

▸ **Date:** Third century

▸ **Location:** Lambayeque Valley, 28 km from Chiclayo (Peru)

▸ **Year Discovered:** 1987

THE LORD OF SIPÁN

He was a powerful Moche ruler from the third century. His clothing and adornment are evidence of his high lineage.

MILITARY LEADER

One of the eight mummies found with the Lord of Sipán. The others are: two young women and an older lady; one child; a standard bearer; a watchman; and a guardian.

Goods Destined for the Beyond

Moche beliefs included faith in another life after death, which the individuals of high rank accessed by carrying goods and wealth when they passed from this life. This included jewels, gold and silver ceremonial items, ceramic vessels, adornments, weapons, and other insignia of power.

Gold Mask. Stylized gold mask with the face of a Moche man, discovered in the tomb.

Buckle. Gold embossed openwork piece with the image of the god Aia Paec. The buckle fastened to a belt.

Breastplate. Made out of Spondylus shells, it alludes to the Lord as a keeper of order.

Teotihuacan

Erected near the current capital of Mexico, it was one of the most populated urban centers in pre-Columbian America. Its name in Nahuatl means "City of the Gods," and it stands out due to its urbanism, influence, and size.

Sacred Orientation

The orientation and distribution of the space in Teotihuacan is based on astronomical calculations. The large avenue that passes through it, the Avenue of the Dead, and all the structures of the city have the same orientation: 16º to the east of astronomical north.

ATETELCO
The murals with warrior themes in this walled area are notable.

AVENUE OF THE DEAD
This "main street" of the city, 4 km long and 40 m wide, connected the Citadel to the Moon Square.

Temple of the Feathered Serpent
Built between 100 and 350 AD, its facade features the heads of serpents, associated with Quetzalcoatl, one of the primary Mesoamerican gods, and aquatic motifs and icons related to Tlaloc, the god of water.

THE CITADEL
Built around 200 BC and possibly the residence of senior dignitaries. There were important religious buildings and a central altar inside the structure's 160,000 m².

TEMPLE OF THE FEATHERED SERPENT

MASKS
The great lords of Teotihuacan were buried with masks to be likened to the gods.

PATIO OF THE JAGUARS
Built between 450 and 650 AD, it contains murals featuring its eponymous feline, as well as snails and feathers to call down rain.

PALACE OF QUETZALPAPALOTL
It is believed that this was the residence of a high-level civil dignitary or a high priest. The name Quetzalpapalotl means "sacred butterfly."

SITE INFORMATION

Type: City	
Date: 200 BC (apogee: 2nd-7th century AD)	
Location: 48 km northeast of Mexico City (Mexico)	
Area: 22 km²	

PYRAMID OF THE MOON

PYRAMID OF THE SUN
Built atop a natural cave where religious rituals were held, this impressive pyramid is 64 m high and measures 250 m on either side. It was built between 1 and 150 AD.

Pyramid of the Moon

It has 242 steps and was built in seven stages. The slope-and-panel structure seen today was built between 200 and 450 AD on top of an older structure similar in design. Stones, adobe, and dirt were used to build it. They also used tepetate (material made from volcanic ash and small compact rocks) and a mix of limestone and clay.

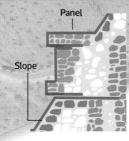

Panel

Slope

 Support slabs

 Finished with sandstone

Core of the pyramid

Structure of the panel

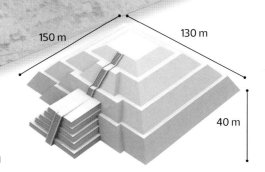

150 m

130 m

40 m

Chichen Itza

This ancestral Maya city, dominated by the great Pyramid of Kukulcan (also known as "the Castle"), has the largest pre-Columbian ball game court in Mesoamerica, a sacred natural cenote used for sacrifices, and an astronomical observatory.

The Great Maya City

Chichen Itza emerged around 450 AD. In the ninth century, it was considered one of the most important Maya political centers, and in the tenth century it was the main center of power of the Yucatán.

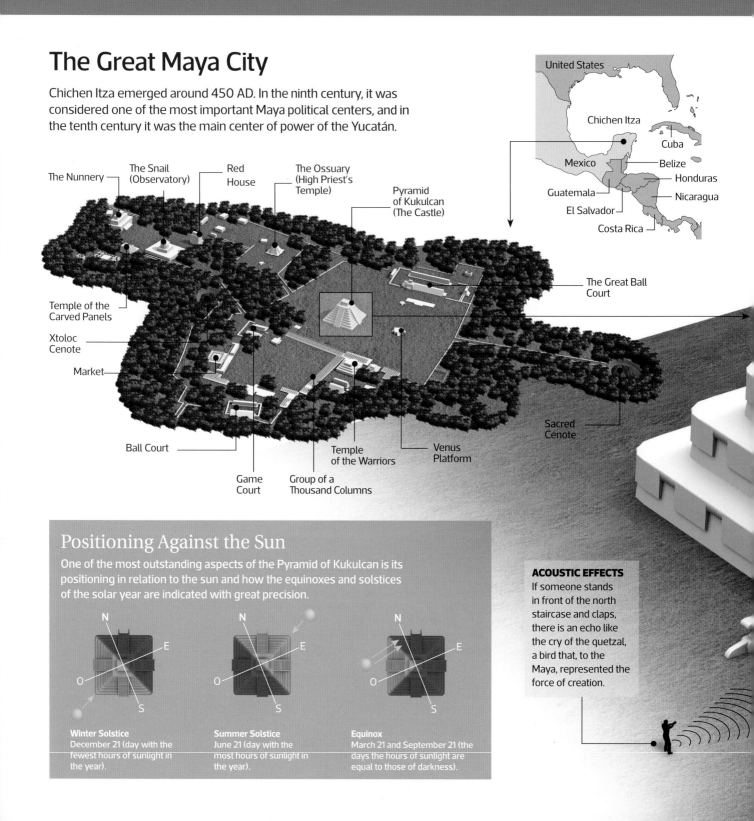

United States
Chichen Itza
Cuba
Mexico — Belize
— Honduras
Guatemala — — Nicaragua
El Salvador —
Costa Rica —

The Nunnery
The Snail (Observatory)
Red House
The Ossuary (High Priest's Temple)
Pyramid of Kukulcan (The Castle)
The Great Ball Court
Temple of the Carved Panels
Xtoloc Cenote
Market
Sacred Cenote
Ball Court
Game Court
Group of a Thousand Columns
Temple of the Warriors
Venus Platform

Positioning Against the Sun

One of the most outstanding aspects of the Pyramid of Kukulcan is its positioning in relation to the sun and how the equinoxes and solstices of the solar year are indicated with great precision.

Winter Solstice
December 21 (day with the fewest hours of sunlight in the year).

Summer Solstice
June 21 (day with the most hours of sunlight in the year).

Equinox
March 21 and September 21 (the days the hours of sunlight are equal to those of darkness).

ACOUSTIC EFFECTS
If someone stands in front of the north staircase and claps, there is an echo like the cry of the quetzal, a bird that, to the Maya, represented the force of creation.

THOUSAND COLUMNS
The Group of a Thousand Columns of Chichen Itza is actually a temple that has around 200 columns.

The Pyramid of Kukulcan
It is the largest temple of Chichen Itza and a masterpiece of Maya architecture. Its refined construction is remarkable.

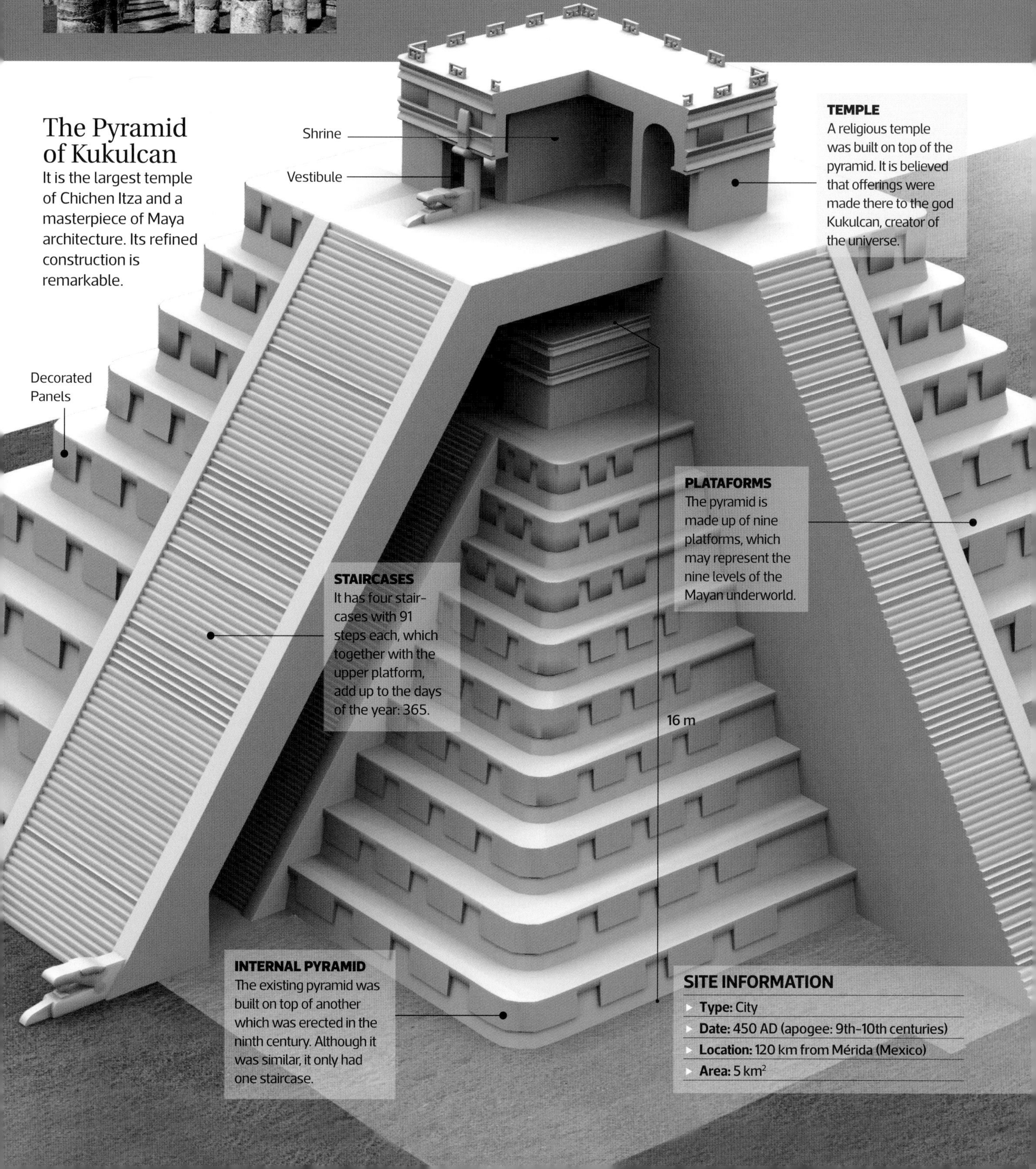

Shrine

Vestibule

TEMPLE
A religious temple was built on top of the pyramid. It is believed that offerings were made there to the god Kukulcan, creator of the universe.

Decorated Panels

PLATAFORMS
The pyramid is made up of nine platforms, which may represent the nine levels of the Mayan underworld.

STAIRCASES
It has four stair-cases with 91 steps each, which together with the upper platform, add up to the days of the year: 365.

16 m

INTERNAL PYRAMID
The existing pyramid was built on top of another which was erected in the ninth century. Although it was similar, it only had one staircase.

SITE INFORMATION
▸ **Type:** City
▸ **Date:** 450 AD (apogee: 9th-10th centuries)
▸ **Location:** 120 km from Mérida (Mexico)
▸ **Area:** 5 km²

The Treasures of the Maya

The Maya were exceptional artists. Masters of color, they gave an original style to their depictions, whether in frescoes, clay figurines, heavy stone stelae, or simple vases and vessels.

Jade, the Most Prized Material

Jade had great symbolic value, and was the most sought-after stone, prized and used by the Maya in their artistic works. The only deposit of this material in Mesoamerica is located in the Motagua River valley of Guatemala. One of the most valuable Maya jade pieces is the mask of Pakal, discovered in the Temple of Inscriptions in Palenque (Mexico). They also created remarkable murals, stone stelae, and clay figurines.

FESTIVITIES
The first chamber at Bonampak portrays a scene of the public presentation of the king, with a procession of musicians.

CENTRAL FIGURE
A centrally-placed drummer with a headdress of feathers separates the two groups of percussion musicians.

Everyday Objects

Maya art appears on all kinds of objects for both ordinary and decorative use, which is a reflection of their lifestyle and culture. Several of the pieces are signed by the artists, who belonged to the elite of Maya society.

VESSEL
Made in Teotihuacan style, it was found in the Margarita Tomb at Copán and belonged to the wife of a king of this Maya city.

JADE ORNAMENT
Delicate chest piece from the Classic Maya period with depiction of a deity, flanked at the top by two heads.

ECCENTRIC
These strange figures, called "eccentric" were made out of flint or obsidian. Human profiles were carved along the edges.

RITUAL CUP
Cylindrical cup from Tikal, in polychrome ceramic, from the Classic period. It is decorated with a scene of members of the aristocracy.

Wooden Art
Bas-relief on a lintel of Temple IV at Tikal. Considered one of the most elaborate pieces of Maya art. Depicts a king on a palanquin.

The Frescoes

The murals are another testimony to the artistic achievements of the Maya. At Bonampak, in the Temple of the Murals, an exquisite display of painting is found (shown in the image). It was preserved through being covered by a layer of calcium carbonate due to water seepage.

MASK OF PAKAL
Belonged to the king of Palenque who ruled in the seventh century. It is made with 340 carefully assembled jade stones. The eyes are made of mother of pearl and obsidian.

EARRING
Ornament made from a seashell, with the image of a warrior, or perhaps a deity. It was worn by both men and women.

Stone Stelae

The tall and heavy stelae are characteristic of the Maya. They usually represent kings or rulers, and almost always include glyphs with historical data, which has served to help us to understand their history better. The best examples were found at Copán.

GUATEMALA

HONDURAS

Copán

Stela D from Copán. This monolith from the beginning of the seventh century depicts the Maya King Uaxaklajuun Ub'aah K'awiil.

Machu Picchu

At an altitude of nearly 2,500 m, this city in the middle of the Andes is the greatest demonstration of Inca architecture and an outstanding example of integration with the environment. It was the royal residence of the ninth Inca King, Pachacuti Inca Yupanqui.

Architectural Jewel

Its buildings carved into the rock, the masonry work (joining the stones without mortar), and perfectly fitted polygonal stone blocks, are outstanding. Its walls, farming terraces, and ramps, designed with the highest level of construction ingenuity, met the challenges of the rugged terrain and adapted to the surrounding natural environment.

INTIWATANA

This sacred place, separated from the main square by 78 steps, served as both an astronomical observatory and an altar where sacrifices were made.

SITE INFORMATION

▷ **Type:** City
▷ **Date:** Fifteenth century
▷ **Location:** 80 km northeast of Cuzco (Peru))
▷ **Year Discovered:** 1911
▷ **City area:** 530 m long by 200 m width

MAIN GATE

The only way to access the city. It is at the end of a long stairway that connects the agricultural and urban areas..

The Forgotten City

The citadel of Machu Picchu was abandoned by the Inca, for unknown reasons, before the arrival of the Spanish. After 300 years in oblivion, the American explorer Hiram Bingham discovered the place for archaeology in 1911.
In the image, the rundown appearance in 1912 of the temple housing the Intiwatana.

The Festival of the Sun

Being an agricultural society, the Incas needed to understand the cycles of nature. In the Temple of the Sun at Machu Picchu, when sunbeams cutting through the east window fall on the sacred stone inside, this means the winter solstice has begun. On that day, the Festival of the Sun was celebrated.

HUAYNA PICCHU
The Inca complex extends to the foot of Huayna Picchu (2,667 m high). It is a landscape of exceptional beauty.

Access

There are several ways to reach the hidden Inca city and the adjacent Huayna Picchu mountain.

1 Modern Road
The winding Hiram Bingham road links the village of Aguas Calientes to Machu Picchu (8 km).

2 Inca Trail
It has become a famous hiking route, 32 km long, taking four days of trekking to get to the city.

3 Huayna Picchu
This mountain, which has its own temples, is accessible from the north end of Machu Picchu.

MAIN SQUARE
It is the only open space in the complex. It was where festivities took place and was also the meeting place of Machu Picchu.

TEMPLE OF THE SUN
Only royalty had access to this temple. The layout of the construction signaled the arrival of the winter solstice.

Chapter 2

Sites in Europe, Asia, and Oceania

A fundamental contribution of archaeology to the knowledge of our past is the verification of myths or information that has been uncorroborated. Its instruments are highly effective at both discarding false data or documents and, conversely, affirming evidence of the authenticity of a site or the existence of an entire civilization. This was the case with the excavations by Arthur Evans on Crete, which revealed the Minoan culture to the world.

Archaeology has proven to be especially useful in the study of material remains of ancient origin. Stonehenge, cave paintings, Çatalhöyük, and other Paleolithic and Neolithic remains in Europe, Asia, and Oceania have proven suitable areas for the further application of experimental archaeology and dating techniques. Questions such as "How were the stones of Stonehenge transported and erected?" can be addressed. In Asia, just four decades ago, it became possible to verify some of the descriptions of Sima Qian—a Chinese historian of the second century BC—regarding the mausoleum of the first emperor of China, Qin Shi Huang. At the same time, one of the greatest findings of the last century was discovered: the terracotta army of the same emperor, in Xi'an.

Paleolithic Venus Figurines

Some 250 small female figurines found at various European archaeological sites attest to artistic progress during the Paleolithic Period as well as to the important role of women in prehistoric societies.

Artistic Evolution

Around 30,000 years ago, stone and bone stopped being primarily raw materials for making tools, and also became the medium for expressing symbolic human thoughts. The small figures known as Paleolithic Venuses are from this first artistic explosion, most of them from the period called the Gravettian culture (30,000–22,000 BC) in Europe.

LOCATION OF PALEOLITHIC VENUSES

Kostenki (Russia)

Dolní Věstonice (Czech Republic)

Marquay (France)

Willendorf (Austria)

Brassempouy (France)

Savignano (Italy)

Grimaldi (Italy)

Lespugue (France)

SYMBOL OF FERTILITY
Many of the figures are of obese women with exaggerated attributes and curves, to extol fertility.

Willendorf Venus

The most famous of the paleolithic Venuses was discovered in Austria and is carved from sandstone. This figure is 11 cm tall and 6 cm wide, and around 25,000 years old.

VENUS OF SAVIGNANO
Carved from soapstone, it was found in 1925 in an alluvial deposit near Modena (Italy). It is 22.5 cm tall and is one of the largest figurines found. Its age is controversial.

KOSTENKI VENUS
This is one of various Venuses found in the Russian site of Kostenki. From 23,000 BC, it is carved from limestone. It is 10.2 cm tall.

VENUS OF LESPUGUE
Found in Haute-Garonne, it is sculpted from ivory and is around 25,000 years old. It had to be reconstructed because it was damaged when it was found.

VENUS OF BRASSEMPOUY
Discovered in the Pope's Cave in 1881 in the French department of Landes. It is carved from mammoth ivory and stands out as being one of the Venuses with the most detailed facial features.

UNDEFINED FACE. This is a common characteristic of almost all of the Paleolithic Venuses.

Venus of Laussel

Carved in relief in a block of limestone, this is a Venus of transition between the Gravettian and Solutrean cultures. It was discovered in Dordogne (France).

Bison horn. The presence of this element in the Venus' hand emphasizes the concept of fertility.

VENUS OF DOLNÌ VĚSTONICE
From a site near the Czech city of Brno, this figure from 25,000 BC is considered by some experts to

THE GRIMALDI VENUSES
This is a set of figures found in the group of caves called Balzi Rossi in the Italian region of Liguria. The

Cave Paintings

Pictorial art first appeared during the Upper Paleolithic period in the form of figurative or abstract representations made on the walls of caves–a medium that has allowed this type of painting to endure over the centuries.

Ritual Art

Although cave art is universal in character, the majority of pictorial manifestations are focused in Europe, where there are over 300 caves with Paleolithic paintings. The most emblematic are those of Lascaux and Chauvet in France and Altamira in Spain. It is believed that this art was somehow connected to a magical-religious influence upon everyday reality –such as drawing an animal before hunting it– or fertility rituals.

Hall of the Bulls. Most of the mammals pictured in this section of Lascaux are females.

ENGRAVINGS AND SCRAPINGS

Many paintings were preceded by an outline of the figure engraved on the surface. Shells were probably used to make them.

LAYOUT OF LASCAUX

Along its 80 meters of walls, the cave has nearly 2,000 paintings and engravings. Half of them are figures of animals: horses, deer, and bison.

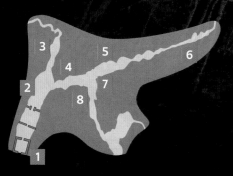

1. Entrance
2. Hall of the Bulls
3.
4.
5. Nave
6. Chamber of Felines
7.
8.

GEOMETRIC SHAPES

An example of shapes –like a checkerboard pattern– which

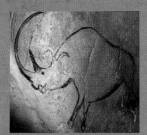

The Chauvet Cave

The cave paintings of Chauvet (France) are among the oldest (32,000 BC) and most beautiful that are known. The drawings of animals, and some humans, are spread across the walls of the cave in wavy patterns.

SITE INFORMATION

▸ **Type:** Cave art in the caves of Lascaux
▸ **Date:** 17,000 BC
▸ **Location:** Montignac, Department of Dordogne (France)
▸ **Year Discovered:** 1940

SUPERIMPOSITION
The superimposed images indicate that the cave had a seasonal use, depending on hunting and the abundance of some species above others.

FEMALES
Most of the mammals pictured on this section of the Hall of the Bulls are pregnant females.

The "Sistine Chapel" Cave

The bison painted in the Altamira cave (Santillana del Mar, Spain) signify a milestone in the intellectual evolution of the human being, earning the site the title of the "Sistine Chapel" of Quaternary art. Discovered in 1879, its authenticity was questioned because it was believed that primitive men were unable to create such stylized artistic depictions of the world around them.

Polychrome.
The colors were obtained from a mixture of animal fats, vegetable juices, blood, eggs, and earth of different shades.

Çatalhöyük

With the Neolithic Revolution and the appearance of agriculture, outstanding stationary establishments were developed, such as Çatalhöyük on the plateau of Anatolia (Turkey), which must have been home to several thousand people.

A Rich and Prosperous Town

The village of Çatalhöyük existed approximately 9,000 years ago. It grew quickly, and it wasn't long before it developed into a rich and prosperous establishment. The site is made up of Neolithic deposits 15 meters deep, grouped into 14 archaeological levels. The levels II to VIII date toward 7000 BC, and are contemporary with the Aceramic Neolithic period of Palestine.

TEXTILES AND LEATHER
Both sun-dried animal skins and woven fabrics were stamped with seals of stone or wood to indicate the name of the owner.

STABLES
Most patios were used as stables. The main diet of the inhabitants consisted of sheep and goat meat, along with wheat and barley.

Construction Techniques

The walls were built with adobe bricks, made from a mixture of mud and straw, and sometimes reinforcement pillars were incorporated. Both the walls and the roof were covered with mud, whereas the interiors were plastered.

The Roofs. They were made with wooden beams and covered with reeds, which rested on pillars.

DUMPSTERS
The objects found in some patios, such as animal remains and broken utensils, suggest their use as garbage dumps.

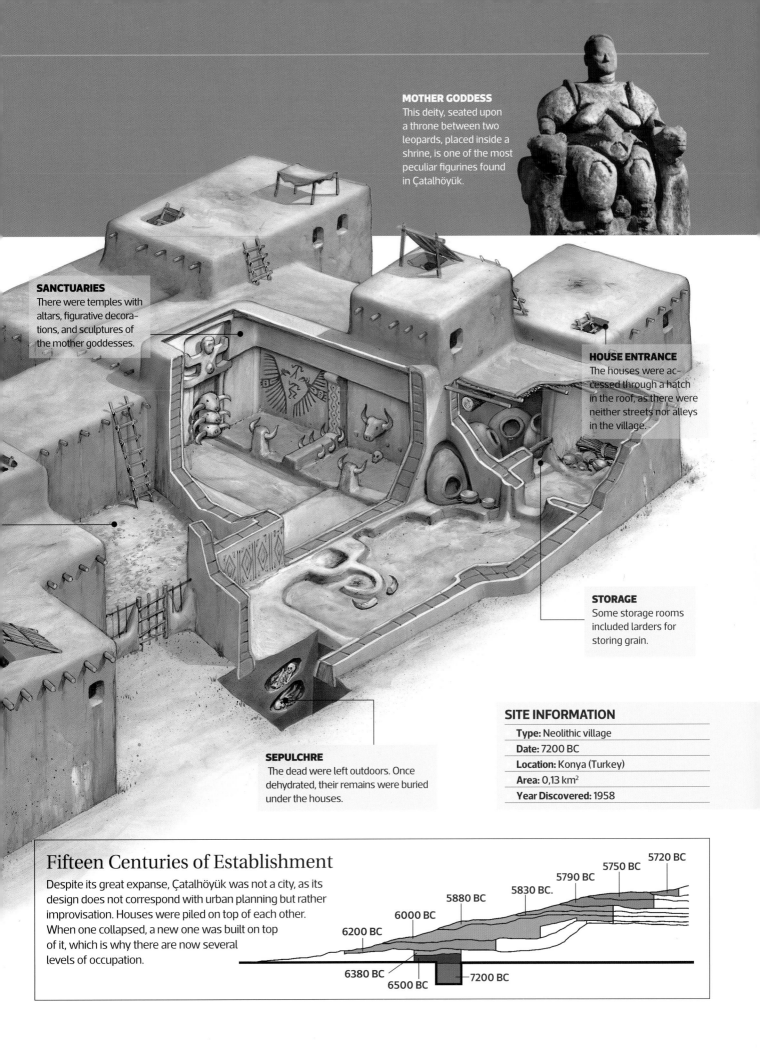

MOTHER GODDESS
This deity, seated upon a throne between two leopards, placed inside a shrine, is one of the most peculiar figurines found in Çatalhöyük.

SANCTUARIES
There were temples with altars, figurative decorations, and sculptures of the mother goddesses.

HOUSE ENTRANCE
The houses were accessed through a hatch in the roof, as there were neither streets nor alleys in the village.

STORAGE
Some storage rooms included larders for storing grain.

SEPULCHRE
The dead were left outdoors. Once dehydrated, their remains were buried under the houses.

SITE INFORMATION

Type: Neolithic village
Date: 7200 BC
Location: Konya (Turkey)
Area: 0,13 km²
Year Discovered: 1958

Fifteen Centuries of Establishment

Despite its great expanse, Çatalhöyük was not a city, as its design does not correspond with urban planning but rather improvisation. Houses were piled on top of each other. When one collapsed, a new one was built on top of it, which is why there are now several levels of occupation.

6200 BC
6000 BC
5880 BC
5830 BC.
5790 BC
5750 BC
5720 BC

6380 BC
6500 BC
7200 BC

Stonehenge

This spectacular complex is a masterful work of European megalithic architecture, erected in the British Islands by a Neolithic society that was very interested in astronomical observation.

Astronomical Calendar

It is believed that Stonehenge was a temple for the observation of astronomical phenomena, a calendar that permitted foretelling the arrival of the seasons to help determine the activities of the peasants and livestock farmers. Most likely, rituals and sacrifices also took place in this location.

The Structure

It is formed by concentric circles of megaliths of up to five meters high. Perfectly positioned on the ground, they can calculate the movement of the sun and the moon and indicate the solstices and eclipses.

FIRST RING

SECOND RING

Sacrificial Stone

MONOLITHS
The large vertical stone blocks, known as menhirs, weigh up to 25 tons.

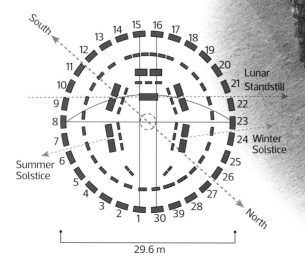

South

15 16
13 14 17 18
12 19
11 20
10 21 Lunar Standstill
9 22
8 23
7 24 Winter Solstice
6 25
Summer Solstice 5 26
4 27
3 2 30 39 28
1 North

29.6 m

Astral Alignment

Every 18.6 years the moon reaches an extreme azimuth on the horizon, the lunar standstill. In Stonehenge, the moon lines up above the sun, reflecting the yearning of the age of hunters that attributed symbolism to the blue heavenly body.

Route traveled by the Sun

Route traveled by the Moon

The Avenue

A processional road 3 km long and 23 m wide, it cuts through the ditch that surrounds the Stonehenge cromlech. It goes by the name "The Avenue" and reaches the Avon River. In the image, an overhead view of Stonehenge and the Avenue.

THIRD RING

FOURTH RING

SITE INFORMATION

- ▶ **Type:** Megalithic monument
- ▶ **Date:** 3100–1100 BC.
- ▶ **Location:** Amesbury, Wiltshire County (United Kingdom)
- ▶ **Diameter:** 104 m (ditch included)

TRILITHONS
These consist of two pillars of stone crowned by a lintel, up to 4.4 meters tall and weighing up to 7 tons.

CRÓMLECH
The circular pattern of menhirs in the megalithic monuments is known as a cromlech.

Ancient Construction

Stonehenge represents a colossal effort of planning and execution. The monument took diverse forms during its long history, spanning about 40 generations.

1 Moving the Stones
The stones were hauled from sur-rounding areas. It is possible that the menhirs brought from Wales were transported by raft on the River Avon.

2 Positioning
Once on the platform, a circular pit was dug into where the stones were pushed using levers and tree trunks.

3 The Menhirs
When the megaliths had been placed in the pit, they were moved upright using ropes and supports, and set into the ground.

4 Positioning of the Lintels
The lintels were raised using a tower of tree trunks. The stones have chiseled protrusions and cavities to ensure a perfect fit with each other.

TYPES OF STONE
The great monoliths are made of sarsen sandstone. The smaller blocks are known as "bluestone" and were brought from Wales.

The Ruins of Mycenae

Between 1600 and 1100 BC, the Achaeans dominated the Eastern Mediterranean with their powerful city-states. Mycenae was the most outstanding of them all, and so this whole civilization was given the title "Mycenaean."

The Kingdom of Agamemnon

The fortified city of Mycenae, with a triangular shape, built on a hill to favor its defense, was initially only a large temple and a small section of wall as of the year 15 BC. It was enlarged around 1250 BC, when the enclosure was completely walled in. According to the stories told by the poet Homer, which speak of the economic and military power of the Achaean people, the city was founded by Perseus, son of Zeus, and governed by King Agamemnon, one of the heroes of the *Iliad*.

The Treasury of Atreus

In the outskirts of Mycenae lies the most famous vaulted tomb in Greece, the Treasury of Atreus. This type of Mycenaean tomb, known as *tholos*, consists of a stone corridor which accesses an underground chamber.

THE "MASK OF AGAMEMNON"
This is the name of the most valuable piece found in Mycenae. It was initially thought that it portrayed the face of King Agamemnon, but it turned out to be from about 300 years prior to the life of the monarch.

Cyclopean Town

The Acropolis of Mycenae is surrounded by an enormous wall, 13 m high and 7 m thick, built with enormous rectangular stone blocks. The main access entrance is the monumental Lion Gate, lions being the symbol of Mycenaean power. Inside the city, the circular cemetery next to the entrance is remarkable, as are the remains of the Palace of Agamemnon, which was sacked in 1200 BC prior to the destruction of the city one century later.

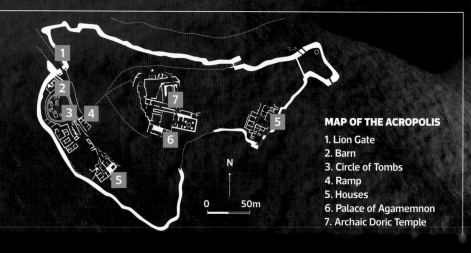

N

0   50m

MAP OF THE ACROPOLIS

1. Lion Gate
2. Barn
3. Circle of Tombs
4. Ramp
5. Houses
6. Palace of Agamemnon
7. Archaic Doric Temple

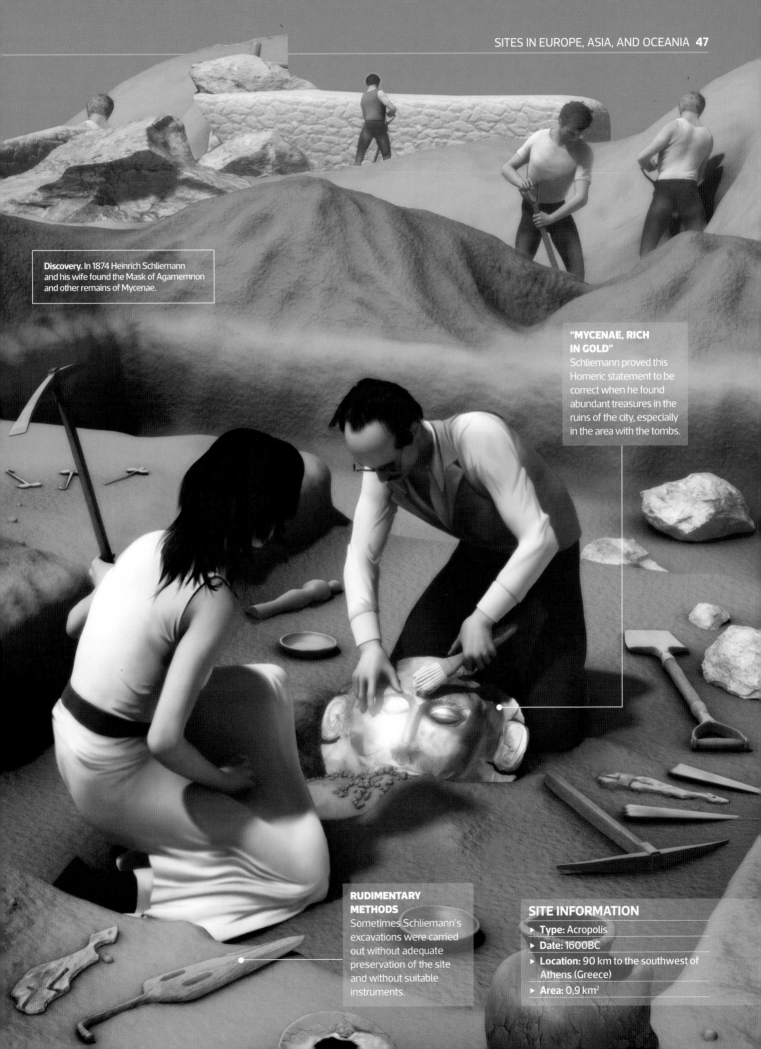

Discovery. In 1874 Heinrich Schliemann and his wife found the Mask of Agamemnon and other remains of Mycenae.

"MYCENAE, RICH IN GOLD"
Schliemann proved this Homeric statement to be correct when he found abundant treasures in the ruins of the city, especially in the area with the tombs.

RUDIMENTARY METHODS
Sometimes Schliemann's excavations were carried out without adequate preservation of the site and without suitable instruments.

SITE INFORMATION

▸ **Type:** Acropolis
▸ **Date:** 1600BC
▸ **Location:** 90 km to the southwest of Athens (Greece)
▸ **Area:** 0,9 km²

Legendary Troy

The ruins of Troy are located beside the Dardanelles Strait, in the region previously known as Asia Minor. Famous due to the Homeric stories, this city became "real" in 1870.

The Myth Made Reality

At the end of the nineteenth century, German archaeologist Heinrich Schliemann, who was a great enthusiast of Homer's epics, made excavations on the hill of Hissarlik, in northwest Turkey, which resulted in the potential discovery of the mythical city of Troy. The ruins showed that there had been different levels or layers of occupation. Schliemann dug up a valuable collection of pieces, known as Priam's Treasure, and believed that it had belonged to the King of Troy, although later dating has disputed this fact.

ALTAR
According to the testimony of Plutarch, Alexander the Great made sacrifices to Athena while visiting Troy.

TROY

Iolcos

AEGEAN
SEA

ASIA
MINOR

Athens

Mycenae

Sparta

Miletus

Rhodes

Knossos

CRETE

The Age of Bronze in the Aegean

In the second millennium BC, Troy reached the height of its power and influence. It maintained significant relations with the Aegean world—which was beginning to be dominated by the great Indo-European invasions, and with the inner kingdoms of Asia Minor, among them the Mitanni Kingdom and the Hittite Empire.

GRECO-ROMAN RUINS
This shrine, located in the south-western zone of the site, belongs to the layers Troy VIII and IX, which are the best preserved.

Homeric Troy

Many historians consider that Troy layer VII corresponds with the city that underwent the siege of the Achaeans for years, around 1250 BC, as Homer relates in the *Iliad*. They cite the ashes and carbonized remains that have been found as a proof.

Trojan War. Achilles on a fifth century BC vase.

WALLS
There are many at the site. Schliemann dug up great walls in the strata corresponding to Troy III and IV.

SITE INFORMATION

▶ **Type:** City
▶ **Date:** 3600 BC (Troy VII: 1250 BC)
▶ **Location:** Beside the Dardanelles Strait, 300 km from Istanbul (Turkey)
▶ **Year Discovered:** 1870

Ten Archaeological Layers

After several excavations, Troy was reconstructed in its ten phases of occupation, which began in the Neolithic Age. A long period of cultural continuity is observed from Troy I to Troy V. Troy VI displays a phase of new splendor of the city and the last levels (VIII, IX, and X) attest to Greek, Roman, and Byzantine presence.

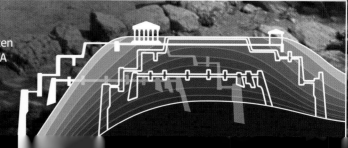

The Parthenon

This immense Greek Doric temple was built in the middle of the fifth century BC at the highest point of the Athens Acropolis. The intent for its construction was to house the statue of Athena Parthenos as well as the accumulated treasures of the city.

Universal Symbol

Without a doubt, the Parthenon of Athens is the best architectonic representation of Greek antiquity. Built by order of Pericles, it has survived numerous attacks and looting throughout history—with great struggle. Its imposing Doric marble columns and the series of sculptures that decorates its outside surface are excceptional.

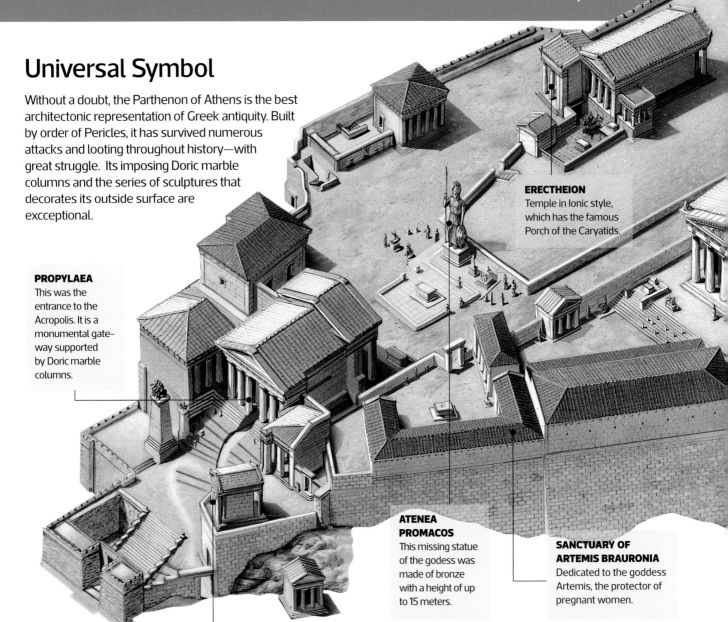

ERECTHEION
Temple in Ionic style, which has the famous Porch of the Caryatids.

PROPYLAEA
This was the entrance to the Acropolis. It is a monumental gate-way supported by Doric marble columns.

ATENEA PROMACOS
This missing statue of the godess was made of bronze with a height of up to 15 meters.

SANCTUARY OF ARTEMIS BRAURONIA
Dedicated to the goddess Artemis, the protector of pregnant women.

TEMPLE OF ATHENA NIKE
Dedicated to Victorious Athena, it is almost square with Ionic design, columns and a frieze with scenes of the victory in the battle against the Persians.

The Plundering of Elgin

At the beginning of the 19th century, the British consul of Constantinople ransacked the Parthenon and other temples, transferring valuable artifacts to his country, which are now on display at the British Museum.

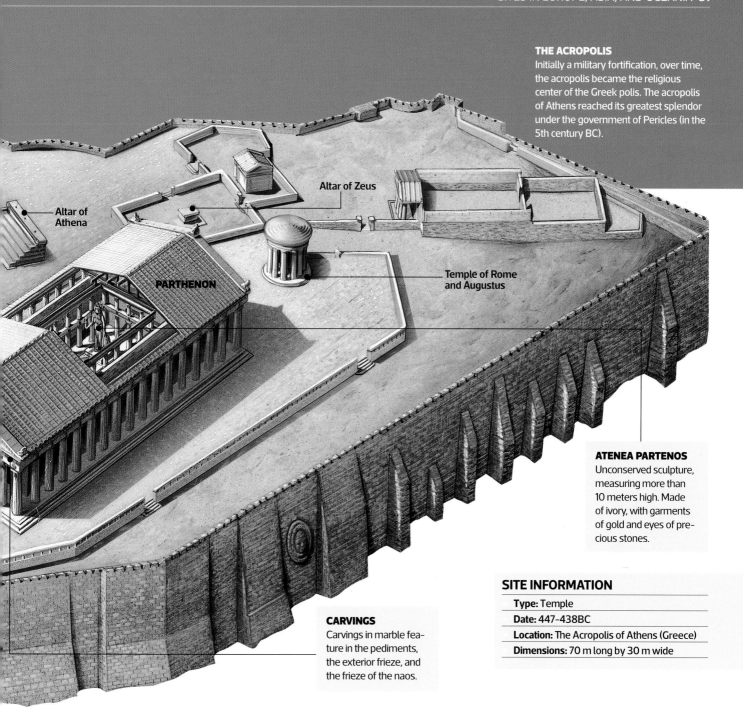

THE ACROPOLIS
Initially a military fortification, over time, the acropolis became the religious center of the Greek polis. The acropolis of Athens reached its greatest splendor under the government of Pericles (in the 5th century BC).

Altar of Zeus

Altar of Athena

PARTHENON

Temple of Rome and Augustus

ATENEA PARTENOS
Unconserved sculpture, measuring more than 10 meters high. Made of ivory, with garments of gold and eyes of precious stones.

CARVINGS
Carvings in marble feature in the pediments, the exterior frieze, and the frieze of the naos.

SITE INFORMATION

Type: Temple	
Date: 447–438BC	
Location: The Acropolis of Athens (Greece)	
Dimensions: 70 m long by 30 m wide	

The Western Canon

As of the seventh century BC, the Greek temples acquired a uniform typology that was to become a prototype for Western religious architecture. The space was organized in a layout derived from old Mycenaean Megara. Around the central hall (naos), where the statue of the divinity was placed, there was an entrance portico (pronaos), another following it (opisthodomos) to store to the offerings, and a colonnade (peristyle) surrounding the entire area.

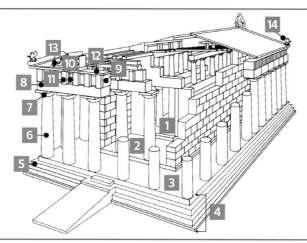

1. Naos
2. Pronaos
3. Peristyle
4. Stereobate
5. Stylobate
6. Shaft
7. Capitel
8. Architrave
9. Frieze
10. Metope
11. Triglyph
12. Cornice
13. Fronton
14. Acroterion

The Ruins of Pompeii

During the first century, Mount Vesuvius buried the city of Pompeii in lava and ashes. Pompeii had been a city of choice for wealthy Romans, as is apparent from its optimally preserved ruins.

Buried Under the Ashes

Thanks to the thick layer of lava and ash from Vesuvius (5 m), the secrets of Pompeii were preserved over the centuries. It was one of the most prosperous Roman cities of its time. The excellent condition of the site, located in 1763, permits viewing of temples, houses with numerous murals, bakeries, laundries, theaters, and taverns of the city, as well as the customs of its inhabitants (12,000-15,0000 people).

THE ERUPTION
At the end of August of the year 79 AD, after days of warning tremors, Vesuvius issued an enormous column of smoke filled with lava and ashes that reached Pompeii in less than 24 hours.

STONE RAIN
Moments after the eruption, incandescent pumice stone bombs began falling.

SITE INFORMATION
▸ **Type:** City
▸ **Date:** First century AD
▸ **Location:** 30 km Southeast of Naples (Italy)
▸ **Year Discovered:** 1763

In Reconstruction

In the year 62, a few years before being devastated by the lava from Vesuvius, Pompeii experienced a great earthquake. When excavating the city, it was verified that many of the buildings were still being refurbished at the time of the eruption.

Ruins of Pompeii. View of the city Forum.

MURALS
Many of the houses in Pompeii were decorated with beautiful frescoes, made with a mix of hot beeswax and color pigments.

WEALTH
The objects found in Pompeii are evidence of the high living standards of the city; it was a vacation destination for the rich Romans.

The End of Pompeii. The illustration portrays the eruption of Vesuvius destroying the city.

A Residential City

Pompeii included 65 hectares of fertile and attractive land that was favored by the climate. Following the Roman scheme, the city grew around its forum, a rectangular area of 142 m x 30 m, located in the town center. The most important religious and civilian public buildings were built around the forum.

1. Basilica
2. Temple of Apollo
3. Treasury of the City
4. Administration Wing
5. Forum
6. Temple of the Triad
7. Residential Wing
8. Building of Eumaquia
9. Temple of Vespasian
10. Shrine of the Lares
11. Market
12. Stores

THE FORUM
This space hosted the city's main political, religious, and commercial activities.

THE HOUSES OF POMPEII
They were extensive houses, with underground heating for some rooms (using steam). The vestibule gave access to the main units. The bedrooms and the kitchen were concentrated in one of the wings of the house.

Exedra. Rectangular hall for welcoming visitors.

Atrium. Room with an opening in the ceiling and a tank for rainwater.

Triclinium. Luxurious dining room, adorned with frescoes and featuring three *klinai* (Roman divans).

Peristyle. Large inner garden, with a porch supported by columns, flowerbeds, and fountains.

The Standard of Ur

This Sumerian masterpiece is about 4,500 years old and was found by British archaeologist Sir Leonard Woolley in the royal necropolis of the ancient city of Ur, South of modern-day Baghdad (Iraq).

Testimony of an Era

The mosaics on the Standard of Ur, the Sumerian city-state in the south of Mesopotamia, portray valuable information about daily life in the Sumerian cities. Thanks to this small wooden object, which was possibly the resonance box of a musical instrument, it is known that the Sumerians were a warrior people who may lived of agriculture and livestock, and maintained a highly hierarchical society.

The Standard of Ur is a trapezoidal wooden box adorned with shells, red limestone, and Lapis Lazuli, attached to the wood with a polish.

THE KING
He is larger in size, representing his position in the hierarchy. He is seated on his throne sporting his finest garments.

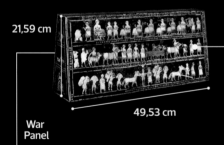

21,59 cm

49,53 cm

War Panel

Peace Panel

Panel of War

In the superior level, the king is shown in the center, surrounded by slaves and prisoners (to the right) and his soldiers (to the left). The central level shows the prisoners with their hands bound, and the triumphant soldiers guarding them. The lower level depicts the battle in progress, which was settled with the commemorated victory.

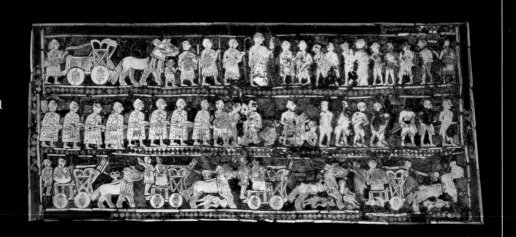

RESTORED
The photographs of both sides of the Standard correspond to a reconstruction of the original one, which is kept in the British Museum.

Panel of Peace

This mosaic, which celebrates a Sumerian military victory, shows the various spoils that were obtained and a banquet where music is played. It emphasizes the character of the king on the upper level, who drinks and converses with the other guests.

The Sumerian Style

The Standard of Ur has certain conventions of artistic representation which are present in both panels of the box.

1 **Front perspective**
The figures are juxta

2 **Hierarchy**
The importance of each

3 **Reading**
The space is framed

SITE INFORMATION

- **Type:** Wooden box with mosaics
- **Date:** 2600–2400 BC
- **Location:** Tell al-Muqayyar, near the mouth of the Euphrates and Tigris rivers (Iraq)
- **Year Discovered:** 1920

Mohenjo-Daro

This fortress-city is the greatest of the cities erected about 4,500 years ago in the lands of the Indus River Valley, which gave rise to the first well-known civilization in the south of Asia.

Pioneers of Urbanism

Mohenjo-Daro is an example of the advanced city planning that the Indus civilization deployed in their cities. It was set from north to south, rectangular, with straight and paved streets, and a sewage system. The residential districts include houses with different numbers of rooms but similar proportions. The ruins were excavated in 1920 by Sir John Marshall, the first archaeologist who defined this civilization, of which Mohenjo-Daro is the main site.

STUPA
The urban center is crowned by a Buddhist stupa of more recent dating than the rest of the city. It was built in the second century BC, atop the mound that had covered the Citadel.

BRICKS
The main material used in the city's construction was baked sun brick, along with wood from the nearby forests.

The Terracotta Records

Multiple terracotta figurines have been found in Mohenjo-Daro and other centers of the

THE CITADEL

Most cities of the Indus civilization had promontories on which the palaces, administrative buildings, and temples were generally built. It was the strongest point of the city, and the place where the ruling class took refuge.

Commerce. The 550 steatite seals found in Mohenjo-Daro were used to mark the merchandise, and have served to confirm the trade that existed with Mesopotamia.

Lower City

The "Lower City" was located on the slopes of the Citadel. This was the area where the residential districts, the craftsmen's workshops, the stores, and the barns of Mohenjo-Daro were located.

Houses and streets. View of one of the residential areas of the "Lower City" of Mohenjo-Daro.

SITE INFORMATION

▸ **Type:** City
▸ **Date:** 2600 BC
▸ **Location:** Larkana (Sind, Pakistan)
▸ **Year Discovered:** 1920

The Priest King

There is no concrete data regarding the religion of the inhabitants of Mohenjo-Daro and the Indus civilization, nor have any representations of their gods been found. Neither are there indications of centralized worship in great temples nor of a religious structure. Nevertheless, it is presumed that a figure that combined political, military, and religious power must have existed. Perhaps for this reason, this statuette, found in the excavations, is known as "the priest king."

GREAT BATH

One of the most outstanding constructions of the compound. It included a great rectangular swimming pool and several concentric rooms.

Mausoleum of Qin Shi Huang

The emperor Qin Shi Huang (260–210 BC), was the first leader to unify China. He left an impressive tomb worthy of his legacy. Within it were three pits filled with thousands of life size soldiers, the now famous army of terracotta warriors.

A Monumental Work

The desire for immortality was an obsession of Qin Shi Huang. Therefore, shortly after assuming the throne, the construction of his monumental mausoleum began. It was a job on which 700,000 people worked at once. The emperor's actual grave is covered by a mound of earth. It has not been excavated. It is assumed that a pyramid with the tomb of the emperor is hidden underneath it.

PIT OF THE BRONZE CARTS
Reproductions of two bronze carts were found here.

HALL OF THE SARCOPHAGUS
According to historian Sima Qian, the emperor's bronze coffin rests in a room of the same material, the floor of which features a map of the land of China, and in which there are rivers of mercury.

HIDDEN PYRAMID
It would be under the mound of earth, which at one point reached 115 meters high. In addition to treasures, the emperor had his concubines, slaves, and animals buried inside it.

Original
115m

Current 47 m

Site of the
Civil Servants

SITE INFORMATION

▸ **Type:** Mausoleum
▸ **Date** Third century BC
▸ **Location:** Mount Li, 30 km from Xi'an (China)
▸ **Area:** 2,1 km²
▸ **Year Discovered:** 1974

Site of the
Acrobats

Chronology of Findings

1974	1976	1980	1998	1999	2000
The discovery of the first pit holding soldiers of the terracotta army, 1.2 km away from the mausoleum.	Skeletons of horses found that had been buried alive in the imperial stables.	Discovery of two bronze carts reproduced to scale, beside the mausoleum.	A ceremonial suit of armor and helmet, decorated with stone tiles, were found.	Discovery of another deposit containing life-sized terracotta human statues.	Site with 12 terracotta civil servants found, and another with 46 different bronze birds.

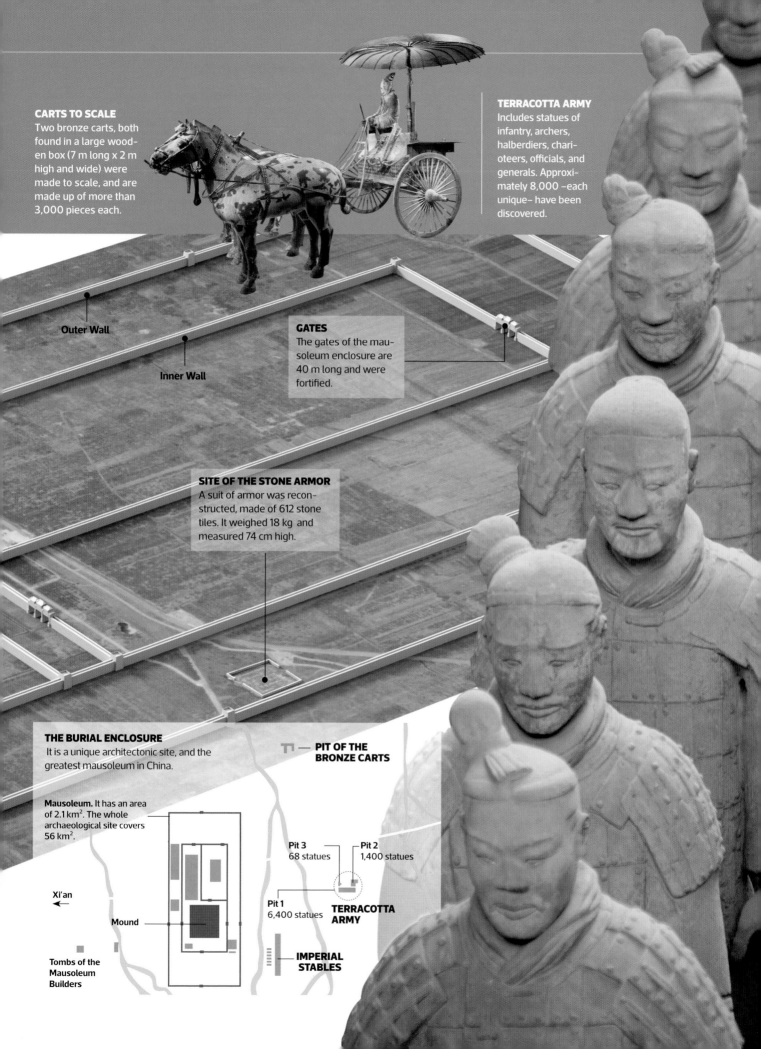

CARTS TO SCALE
Two bronze carts, both found in a large wooden box (7 m long x 2 m high and wide) were made to scale, and are made up of more than 3,000 pieces each.

TERRACOTTA ARMY
Includes statues of infantry, archers, halberdiers, charioteers, officials, and generals. Approximately 8,000 –each unique– have been discovered.

Outer Wall

Inner Wall

GATES
The gates of the mausoleum enclosure are 40 m long and were fortified.

SITE OF THE STONE ARMOR
A suit of armor was reconstructed, made of 612 stone tiles. It weighed 18 kg and measured 74 cm high.

THE BURIAL ENCLOSURE
It is a unique architectonic site, and the greatest mausoleum in China.

⊓ — **PIT OF THE BRONZE CARTS**

Mausoleum. It has an area of 2.1 km². The whole archaeological site covers 56 km².

Xi'an

Mound

Tombs of the Mausoleum Builders

Pit 3
68 statues

Pit 2
1,400 statues

Pit 1
6,400 statues

TERRACOTTA ARMY

IMPERIAL STABLES

The Ruins of Qumran

It is not certain who originally inhabited this old citadel or what its purpose was, but it is known to have been occupied by the Romans toward its end. Its possible connection with the famous Dead Sea Scrolls, found in numerous caves nearby, is yet to be ascertained.

The Citadel

It is about 2 km away from the Western coast of the Dead Sea, atop a cliff. It is likely to have been a monastic retreat. The walls were destroyed by the Romans. A layer of ash covers the ruins, in which a large number of arrowheads were found.

SITE INFORMATION

Type: Citadel

Date: Third century BC

Location: Western coast of the Dead Sea, 13 km from Jericho (Palestine)

Year Discovered: 1951-56

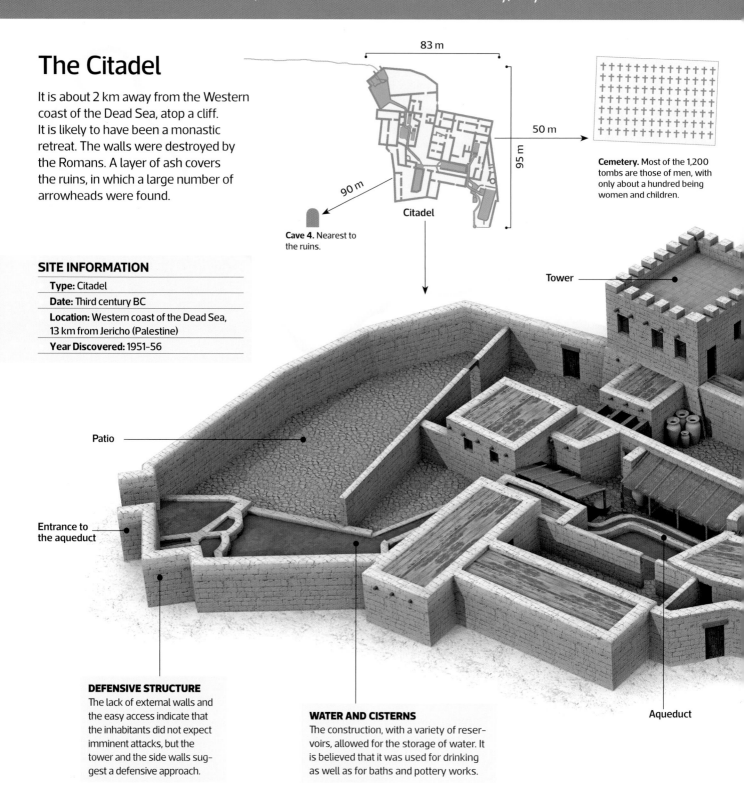

83 m

50 m

95 m

90 m

Cave 4. Nearest to the ruins.

Citadel

Cemetery. Most of the 1,200 tombs are those of men, with only about a hundred being women and children.

Tower

Patio

Entrance to the aqueduct

Aqueduct

DEFENSIVE STRUCTURE
The lack of external walls and the easy access indicate that the inhabitants did not expect imminent attacks, but the tower and the side walls suggest a defensive approach.

WATER AND CISTERNS
The construction, with a variety of reservoirs, allowed for the storage of water. It is believed that it was used for drinking as well as for baths and pottery works.

The Scriptorium

One of the central rooms used in the everyday life of those inhabiting the establishment. It is presumed that papyri rolls and parchments were written and stored here.

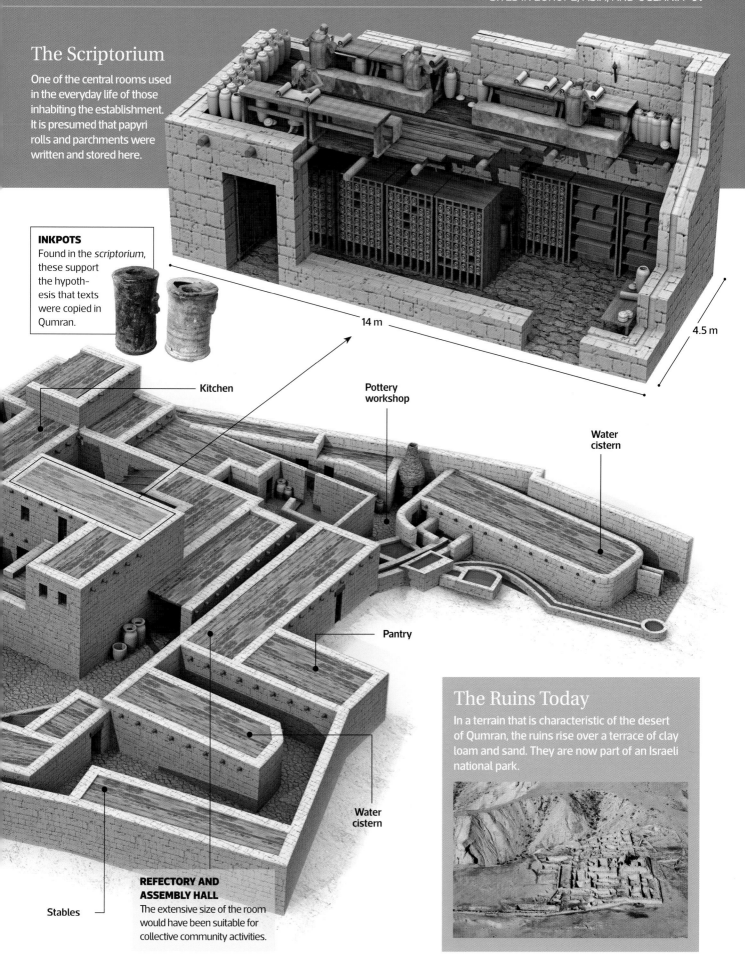

INKPOTS
Found in the *scriptorium*, these support the hypothesis that texts were copied in Qumran.

14 m

4.5 m

Kitchen

Pottery workshop

Water cistern

Pantry

Water cistern

The Ruins Today

In a terrain that is characteristic of the desert of Qumran, the ruins rise over a terrace of clay loam and sand. They are now part of an Israeli national park.

REFECTORY AND ASSEMBLY HALL
The extensive size of the room would have been suitable for collective community activities.

Stables

The Moai of Easter Island

The enormous and mysterious volcanic rock sculptures known as moai, about 900 carved monoliths in total, scattered around Easter Island, are the main remnant of the first inhabitants of the place –the Rapanui people.

The Legacy of the Rapanui

On April 5, 1722, Easter Sunday, the Dutch sailor Jacob Roggeveen landed on a small triangular island in the Pacific Ocean. He came across a rudimentary town with few resources, a small settlement of Rapanui people, and a large quantity of gigantic statues—the moai—most of them toppled, and aligned along the coast on enormous stone platforms.

Route
Track or Trail
⊙ **Urban Center**
◉ **Moai Zone**

North Cape

Point San Juan

PACIFIC OCEAN

Point Rosalia

EASTERN ISLAND

Hanga Roa

ORONGO
Petroglyphs were pre-served in the rocks found in this Ceremonial Center.

RANO RARAKU VOLCANO
It is 100 m high and has a lake inside it. The outer slope and the crater formed the quarry from which the moai were carved.

South Cape

Chilean Sea

Hoa Hakananai'a
This unique moai was found in a house in the ceremonial center of Orongo. Today it is in the British Museum. It weighs four tons and measures 2.5 m high. Like other moai, its torso is carved, although this one stands out because of its engraved designs, related to the birdman cult.

AHU
There are 288 moai connected to ahu –the platforms where the statues were placed– and the rest are throughout the island.

Anatomy of the Moai

The sculptures share certain characteristics, although none of them is identical. All are carved from rock, they are sometimes crowned by a hat (pukao) of red scoria, and some have eyes. On average, they measure 4 m and weigh 12 tons.

AHU KO TE RIKU
The Ko Te Riku Moai, the only one found still standing on its *ahu*, measures 5.2 m and is thought to have been carved in the ninth century.

PUKAO
58 moai wear a topknot, the average weight of which is 10 tons. It is believed that it represents either a hairdo or a hat.

MATERIAL
Carved from volcanic rock, most of the moai are made of tuff, although there are ten made of basalt.

EYES
Are sometimes made of coral or obsidian, and in some cases painted. All are restored, since the incrustations had been lost.

AHU TONGARIKI
This is the largest *ahu* on the island, with 15 moai statues.

e Perouse
ay

Cabo
O'Higgins

Cape
Cumming

5.2 m

Moai Ko Te Riku

SITE INFORMATION
▶ **Type:** Monolithic sculptures
▶ **Date:** Tenth to sixteenth centuries
▶ **Location:** Easter Island, region of Valparaiso (Chile), in the Pacific Ocean
▶ **Year Discovered:** 1722

Archaeology and Its Methodology

Chapter 3

Some archaeological finds are the result of purposeful searches lasting years or even centuries. Others, however, are the result of luck, occurring during excavations seeking something else, or sometimes during the construction of a modern building. It is undeniable that the tenacity of some archaeologists has had a great impact on archaeological finds throughout history. Howard Carter (1874–1939) searched tirelessly for years for Tutankhamen's tomb; Heinrich Schliemann's (1822–1890) obsession with Troy and Mycenae led him to track their ruins—with the verses of The *Iliad* and the writings of Pausanias in hand—until both were found. Over time, these famous discoverers, mainly archaeology enthusiasts who employed destructive excavation methods, gave way to generations of ever-more prepared archaeologists, for whom technology came to provide an enormous number of new resources. Satellite images, aerial and infrared photography, DNA identification, advances in dating chemistry, the study of remains and the environment, and even robotics, have completely transformed archaeology and accelerated the pace of its advances into the study of our past.

What Is Archaeology?

It is a science dedicated to the study of materials from the past. It is the only significant source of information for most of the history of mankind, which began about three million years ago, but has no written sources until about the third millennium BC.

Explaining the Past

The purpose of archaeology is to research what life was like in the past through material remains—what our ancestors ate, how they dressed, what their beliefs were, how their social organization was structured, what changes occurred in the environment, among other aspects. Several methods are used for collecting data, although the most significant is excavation, which exposes archaeological remains that had been buried over time.

Phases of Archaeological Excavation

1 Exploration and Excavation
After exploring an area and its layers, the excavation proceeds and horizontal and vertical records are made of the location.

2 Measurements and Cleaning
The objects and materials extracted are analyzed and measured, and when necessary cleaned using brushes.

3 Laboratory Work
Next, the diverse remains found are classified and taken to the laboratory. Reports are prepared.

4 Absolute Dating
Carbon-14 and rehydroxylation are among the techniques used to determine the date of the archaeological remains and provide accurate information.

5 Publication and Dissemination
The results are published in print and digital media. The most outstanding pieces, like this ninth-century Viking ship, are showcased in museums.

Cape Nome
Onion Portage
Bluefish Caves
Dry Creek
Kennewick
Yuquot
Mesa Verde
Ballynacree
Carrier Mills
Hopewell
Ozette
Lindenmeier
Azatlan
Draper
Chaco Canyon
Cahokia
Meadowcroft Rockshelter
Gatecliff Shelter
Folsom
Domebo
Koster
Adena Mound
Snaketown
Clovis
Moundville
Lehner
Tula
Teotihuacan
Tenochtitlan
Poverty Point
Chichen Itza
Caddo Mounds
Tehuacán
Tulum
Guila Naquitz
El Mirador
Tikal
Copán
San José Mogote
Monte Albán
Palenque
San Lorenzo
La Venta
Chavín de Huántar
Moche
Sipán
Gruta Pedra Pintada
Chan Chan
Guitarrero Cave
El Paraíso
Huanuco Pampa
Machu Picchu
Nazca
Cusco
Eastern Island
Quebrada Tacahuay
Monte Verde
Cueva Fell

FELL CAVE (ARGENTINA)
In 1936, remains of the oldest human settlement were found in Tierra del Fuego (11,000 BC).

TIWANAKU (BOLIVIA)
A city established by a 2000-1500 BC pre-Inca culture.

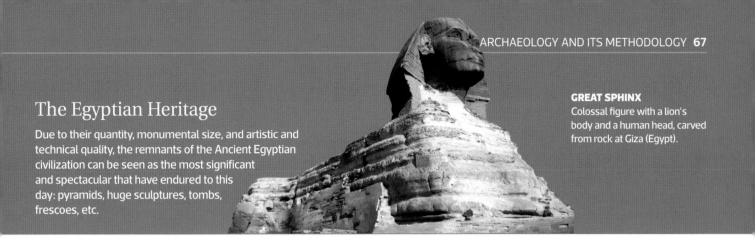

The Egyptian Heritage

Due to their quantity, monumental size, and artistic and technical quality, the remnants of the Ancient Egyptian civilization can be seen as the most significant and spectacular that have endured to this day: pyramids, huge sculptures, tombs, frescoes, etc.

GREAT SPHINX
Colossal figure with a lion's body and a human head, carved from rock at Giza (Egypt).

Sites and Findings

The map shows places where valuable remains of ancient civilizations have been found: caves, temples, tombs, villages, whole cities ...

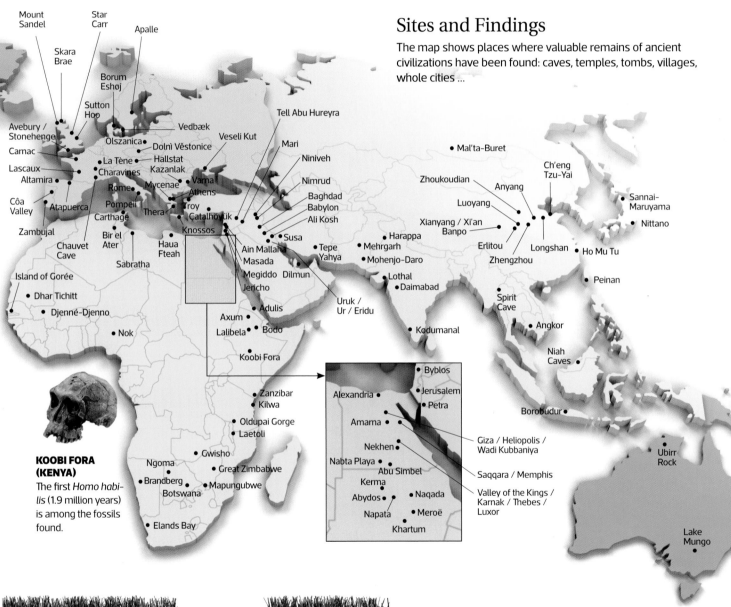

Mount Sandel
Star Carr
Apalle
Skara Brae
Borum Eshøj
Sutton Hoo
Avebury / Stonehenge
Carnac
Lascaux
Altamira
Côa Valley
Zambujal
Island of Gorée
Dhar Tichitt
Djenné-Djenno
Nok
Olszanica
Vedbæk
Veseli Kut
Tell Abu Hureyra
Dolnì Věstonice
La Tène
Hallstat
Kazanlak
Charavines
Rome
Mycenae
Varna
Athens
Troy
Çatalhöyük
Pompeii
Thera
Knossos
Carthage
Bir el Ater
Haua Fteah
Sabratha
Chauvet Cave
Atapuerca
Mari
Niniveh
Nimrud
Baghdad
Babylon
Ali Kosh
Ain Mallaha
Masada
Megiddo
Dilmun
Jericho
Axum
Lalibela
Bodo
Adulis
Koobi Fora
Susa
Tepe Yahya
Uruk / Ur / Eridu
Mal'ta-Buret
Zhoukoudian
Ch'eng Tzu-Yai
Anyang
Sannai-Maruyama
Luoyang
Nittano
Xianyang / Xi'an
Banpo
Harappa
Mehrgarh
Erlitou
Longshan
Ho Mu Tu
Mohenjo-Daro
Zhengzhou
Lothal
Daimabad
Peinan
Spirit Cave
Kodumanal
Angkor
Niah Caves
Zanzibar
Kilwa
Oldupai Gorge
Laetoli
Gwisho
Ngoma
Great Zimbabwe
Brandberg
Mapungubwe
Botswana
Elands Bay
Borobudur
Ubirr Rock
Lake Mungo

Byblos
Alexandria
Jerusalem
Petra
Amarna
Nekhen
Giza / Heliopolis / Wadi Kubbaniya
Nabta Playa
Abu Simbel
Saqqara / Memphis
Kerma
Abydos
Naqada
Valley of the Kings / Karnak / Thebes / Luxor
Napata
Meroë
Khartum

KOOBI FORA (KENYA)
The first *Homo habilis* (1.9 million years) is among the fossils found.

Interpretation

The remains that are found reveal different aspects of a civilization: its evolutionary, technological, and social development; diet, level of wealth, building techniques used, etc. The archaeological layer in which it was found indicates the period to which it belonged.

Construction: technological progress, social organization.

Seeds: food, agriculture, climate.

Organic Remains: food, climate.

Bones: evolutionary development, diseases.

Coins: commercial and social development.

Ceramics: technological development, customs.

Great Archaeologists

Archaeology as a science only has around two centuries of history, and its development has been impressive. Both amateurs and professionals have made significant discoveries.

Names for History

The list of archaeologists who have made discoveries of treasures or of scientific interest is very long. However, because of the dramatic nature or significance of their discoveries, some have left indelible footprints, including: Carter, discoverer of Pharaoh Tutankhamen's tomb, and Schliemann and Bingham, who located the cities of Troy and Machu Picchu, respectively.

Hiram Bingham

(1875-1956). An American explorer and political activist, he located the citadel of Machu Picchu in Peru, as well as other important archaeological sites in the Sacred Valley of the Inca (Choquequirao, Vitcos and Vilcabamba).

Heinrich Schliemann

(1822-1890). After making a fortune in business, this German archaeology enthusiast dedicated himself to search for the ruins of Troy, which he located in Hissarlik (Turkey) in 1870. Schliemann, who later also excavated Mycenae, has the distinction of having located the mythical city of the *Iliad*.

The Leakey Family

Thanks to the discoveries of the British couple Louis and Mary Leakey in 1959, it was found out that Humanity's origins lay in Africa. Both found further remains of enormous significance toward the understanding of pre-history, as did their son, Richard.

Zahi Hawass

(1947). This high-profile Egyptologist identified the mummy of Queen Hatshepsut, discovered new passages in the Great Pyramid, and directed the CT scan performed on Tutankhamen's mummy.

Howard Carter

(1873-1939). He began working in Egypt at only 17 years old, copying Pharaonic inscriptions, recordings, and paintings. In 1922, he discovered Tutankhamen's tomb, virtually unaltered. He had previously located the tombs of Pharaoh Thutmose IV and Queen Hatshepsut.

THE VALUE OF THE DISCOVERY
Tutankhamen's tomb is the only Egyptian burial enclosure that was preserved practically unaltered for thousands of years.

ENORMEOUS TASK
Carter spent ten years classifying objects from the tomb, and was not able to finish his report of several volumes.

The Fathers of Archaeology

Ciriaco de Ancona
(c. 1391-1455). Considered as the "first archaeologist in history," he left detailed descriptions and drawings of ancient ruins.

Johann Winckelmann
(1717-1768). He modernized archaeology by improving scientific rigor in excavations and the preservation and documentation of remains.

Augustus Pitt Rivers
(1827-1900). His classification method for archaeological materials, not limited solely to the most valuable objects, was innovative.

William M. F. Petrie
(1853-1942). Applied renewed focus on excavation and classification systems. Developed the dating system of seriation.

Dame K. Kenyon
(1906-1978). Developed the Wheeler-Kenyon method; a technique of excavating by sections within a grid.

Carbon-14 Dating

Developed in 1949 by Willard Libby (Winner of the Nobel Prize in Chemistry in 1960) and perfected in 1977 with the introduction of particle accelerator mass spectrometry, carbon-14 dating is a very reliable method for dating organic remains as old as 60,000 years.

Loss of Carbon

All organisms absorb carbon throughout their lifetime. When they die, their organic remains lose this carbon at a regular constant rate, which allows the existence of the living being to be dated. Accelerator mass spectrometry (AMS) can analyze very small samples.

What Are Isotopes?

Isotopes are atoms that have identical numbers of protons, but different numbers of neutrons. Carbon has 3 isotopes: 12C, 13C and 14C. Carbon 14 is radioactive, as it disintegrates over time. This molecule allows materials to be dated.

$^{12}C^-$

$^{13}C^-$

2 Magnetic Deflector

The magnetic deflector performs the first separation of negative ions, alternately injecting equivalent masses. The carbon 14 ions and hydrogen carbonate molecules are directed to the accelerator. Other particles are deflected and blocked by the magnetic device.

Terminal

Electric lenses
Focus the ion beam.

1 Ionization of the Sample

This is achieved by bombarding it with electrons. Cesium is used for this process, which donates its electrons to the sample, forming negative carbon ions. The result is a plasma that is inserted into the conduit.

Conduit

Ion pre-accelerator.
Directs the carbon ions

The Shroud of Turin

Laboratories from three universities were chosen to date the shroud: Arizona, Oxford, and the Polytechnic Institute of Zurich. The sample consisted of a 7cm piece, which was then divided into three sections, each weighing around 50 mg.

Sample size

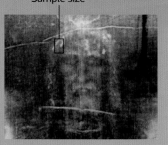

Other Methods

Dating of materials can also be performed using other scientific techniques.

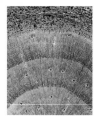

Dendrochronology

This dating system is based on the analysis of tree rings. Each tree produces one ring per year of different widths depending on climatic conditions.

Rehydroxylation

This technique is used to date ceramics. It measures the water that has been reabsorbed by the clay since its first firing.

SPECTROMETER

A student using a mass spectrometer at the Alexander Fleming Biomedical Sciences Research Center in Athens (Greece).

Drawbacks of the Method

One drawback of this dating system is that it assumes that the production of carbon-14 in the atmosphere was constant over the last 60,000 years; whereas there have been fluctuations in different periods and places that must be taken into account. The samples could also have been contaminated after the death of a living being, resulting in a date that makes the sample appear younger than it really is.

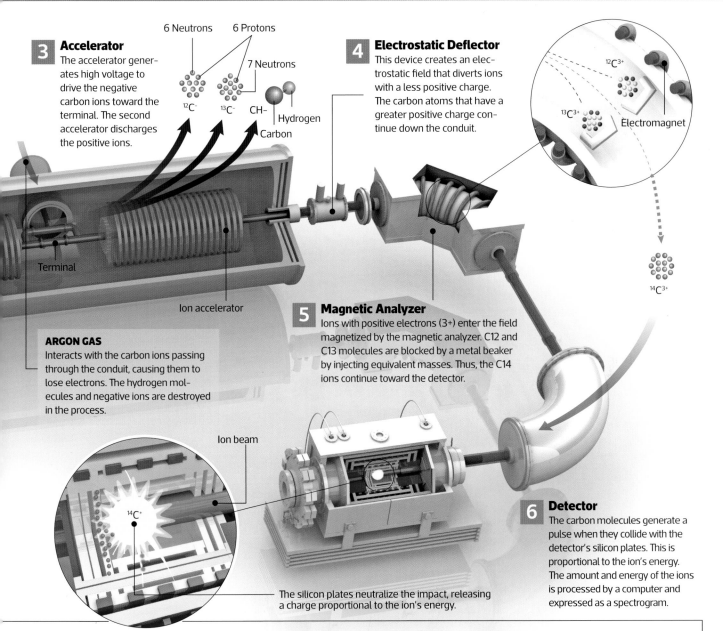

3 Accelerator
The accelerator generates high voltage to drive the negative carbon ions toward the terminal. The second accelerator discharges the positive ions.

6 Neutrons 6 Protons
7 Neutrons
$^{12}C^-$ $^{13}C^-$ CH^-
Hydrogen
Carbon

4 Electrostatic Deflector
This device creates an electrostatic field that diverts ions with a less positive charge. The carbon atoms that have a greater positive charge continue down the conduit.

$^{12}C^{3+}$
$^{13}C^{3+}$ Electromagnet
$^{14}C^{3+}$

Terminal

Ion accelerator

ARGON GAS
Interacts with the carbon ions passing through the conduit, causing them to lose electrons. The hydrogen molecules and negative ions are destroyed in the process.

5 Magnetic Analyzer
Ions with positive electrons (3+) enter the field magnetized by the magnetic analyzer. C12 and C13 molecules are blocked by a metal beaker by injecting equivalent masses. Thus, the C14 ions continue toward the detector.

Ion beam

$^{14}C^+$

The silicon plates neutralize the impact, releasing a charge proportional to the ion's energy.

6 Detector
The carbon molecules generate a pulse when they collide with the detector's silicon plates. This is proportional to the ion's energy. The amount and energy of the ions is processed by a computer and expressed as a spectrogram.

Potassium–Argon
Like radiocarbon dating, this technique is based on the radioactive disintegration produced by the gradual changing of the potassium 40 isotope to argon 40.

Uranium 238
Radiometric system, also called fission track dating. This method allows materials to be dated to billions of years back.

Thermoluminescence
This technique measures the radiation emitted by crystalline structures in inorganic materials in a time range similar to carbon-14 dating.

How the Ground Is Explored

Analysis of the soil makes it possible to ascertain its fertility, which is very useful for archaeology, especially in regions rich in strata. For example, soil composition can reveal its capacity for providing nourishment to groups of people in the past.

Composition Analysis

To determine the composition, fertility, and health of soil, its physical, chemical, and biological properties are analyzed. Important physical parameters include structural stability, moisture retention, texture, and porosity. Important chemical properties include acidity based on pH levels, carbon relation, salts, metals, and other elements. Biological parameters that are measured include the presence of organic matter and worms, and microbial activity.

In the Laboratory

After being logged, the samples are allowed to dry and are then ground and sieved. They are then chemically analyzed to determine pH (pH meter) and the amount of phosphorus (solutions), sodium and potassium (photometry), and calcium and magnesium (complexometry).

Sample Procedure

1 Preparation

A homogeneous sample area is selected, and a sample extraction process is established: for example, every 20 feet in a zigzag pattern.

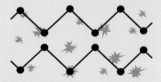

2 Excavation

After clearing the sample area's surface, a V-shaped opening is dug with a shovel, and a section of earth 5 or 6 cm thick is taken.

3 Subsample

The sides of the section are removed using a machete, leaving a piece 5 cm wide (the subsample), which is placed in the bucket. Between 15 and 20 samples per hectare are taken.

4 Mixing

The subsamples are mixed well in the bucket, and a 1 kg portion is placed in a bag and sent to the laboratory for analysis.

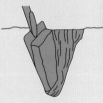

Tools Without Contaminants

Obtaining soil samples does not require specialized tools: a shovel and a bucket will often do, or for more sophisticated samples, a drill or extracting device. However, it is essential that the tools are clean before they are used. The presence of products such as fertilizers or fuel could contaminate the samples and invalidate the results of the analysis.

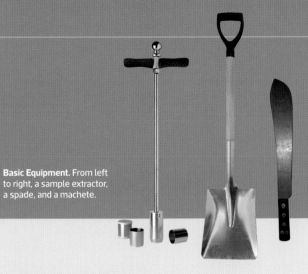

Basic Equipment. From left to right, a sample extractor, a spade, and a machete.

Soil Age Analysis

Learning the age of soil, when it is of anthropogenic origin (meaning it has been affected by human intervention) is an archaeologist's concern. The presence of organic material, such as charcoal, allows the sample to be dated using the carbon-14 method. The presence of ceramics or stratigraphic signs can also be used as a guide.

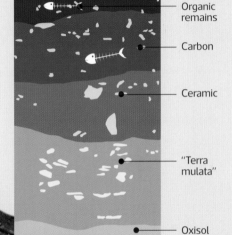

"TERRA PRETA" STRATA
This type of soil, from the Amazon basin, is one of the richest in strata.

- Organic remains
- Carbon
- Ceramic
- "Terra mulata"
- Oxisol

MEASURING
Measuring the depth of each layer is one of the essential procedures.

Archaeology from the Sky

Thanks to aerial photography, taken from satellites in space or from aircrafts, geoglyphs and structures that have been hidden due to the passage of time can now be discovered.

Aerial Reconnaissance

The field of aerial archaeology began with the first hot-air balloons (at the end of the eighteenth century) and the invention of photography (some decades later). This field became a very important tool for discovering and studying the remains of past civilizations that, due to erosion or the growth of vegetation, are no longer visible. Thanks to this field, geoglyphs such as those on the Nazca Plains were discovered.

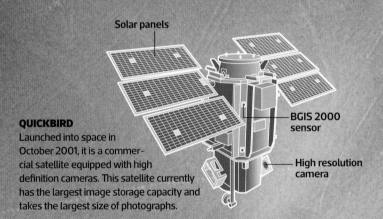

Solar panels

BGIS 2000 sensor

High resolution camera

QUICKBIRD
Launched into space in October 2001, it is a commercial satellite equipped with high definition cameras. This satellite currently has the largest image storage capacity and takes the largest size of photographs.

Discovering Cahuachi

In October 2008, a team of Italian researchers discovered a pyramid, a ceremonial center of the Nazca culture, buried near the desert of Cahuachi (right), close to where other similar formations had already been found. They discovered it using multi-spectral images (including red and infrared wavelengths).

Indications. In this infrared image, the black arrows indicate man-made structures, the red ones indicate an ancient channel of the Nazca River, and the white ones indicate the position of a pyramid buried underground.

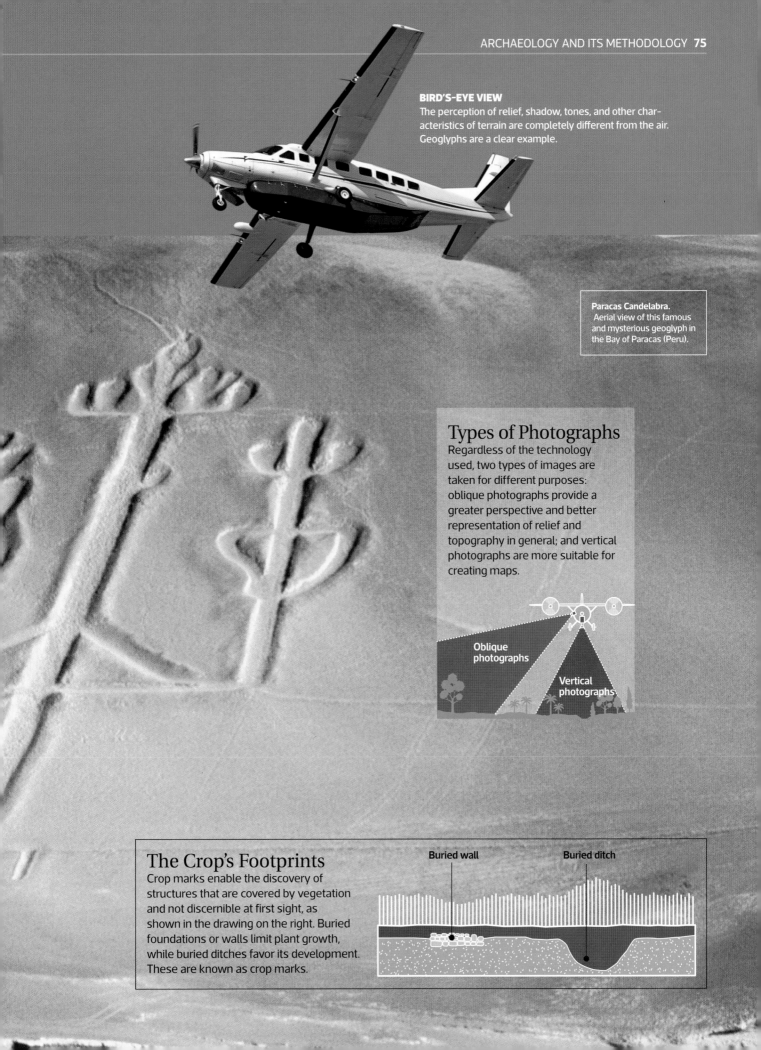

BIRD'S-EYE VIEW
The perception of relief, shadow, tones, and other characteristics of terrain are completely different from the air. Geoglyphs are a clear example.

Paracas Candelabra.
Aerial view of this famous and mysterious geoglyph in the Bay of Paracas (Peru).

Types of Photographs
Regardless of the technology used, two types of images are taken for different purposes: oblique photographs provide a greater perspective and better representation of relief and topography in general; and vertical photographs are more suitable for creating maps.

Oblique photographs

Vertical photographs

The Crop's Footprints
Crop marks enable the discovery of structures that are covered by vegetation and not discernible at first sight, as shown in the drawing on the right. Buried foundations or walls limit plant growth, while buried ditches favor its development. These are known as crop marks.

Buried wall

Buried ditch

Underwater Archaeology

This discipline focuses on the recovery of submerged remains from the past. The main objective is to locate vessels of any kind that have shipwrecked, resulting in numerous archaeological remains dispersed across the seabed.

History Submerged

The invention of autonomous diving equipment enabled underwater archaeology to advance since the middle of the last century. It has also needed contributions from other professionals such as geologists, restoration professionals, chemists, and documentary specialists. This specialization helps to provide in-depth information about past battles, ancient submerged ruins and ports, trade exchange from other eras, and even the lives of the crew and passengers of shipwrecked vessels.

Assistive Technology

To explore places inaccessible to divers due to depth or lack of space, small remotely operated submarines are used, such as the *Triggerfish* (image), equipped with two halogen lamps of 150 watts each with a 300 m range video camera.

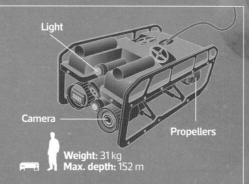

Light

Camera

Propellers

Weight: 31 kg
Max. depth: 152 m

FAVORABLE CONDITIONS
Due to the low level of oxygen and minimized action of chemicals in water, non-metallic archaeological remains are better preserved in this medium.

Conservation of the Findings

The major challenge faced by this discipline is to conserve the remains that are found. When objects are taken from the sea, their balance with the environment is broken, sparking physiochemical processes that can accelerate the decomposition process. It is therefore essential that samples are transported to the restoration laboratory by specialists.

FINDING FROM THE TITANIC
Original bell from the legendary Titanic, which sank in 1912 in North Atlantic waters. Its wreck was found in 1985 by Robert Ballard.

SELECTION
Only objects for which conservation can be guaranteed in the air should be extracted. Otherwise, it is advisable to maintain the object *in situ*.

Shipwreck. A diver recovers wreckage from a ship that sank in 1025 in the Bay of Serçe Limani (Turkey).

Organization and Tools

Tasks are usually distributed between four teams: one on the surface, in a vessel vertically aligned with the site; the auxiliary team at a nearby beach, controlling logistics; the receiving team, for conserving objects; and the sub-aquatic team, made up of divers who explore the site. These are some tools used by divers:

NOTEBOOK
In situ records are essential. Special pens and laminated paper on which the pens can write are used for taking notes.

LIFTING BAG
Remains (or sediments) that are too large to be carried by the diver are raised using a lifting device.

GRID
A portable grid enables the archaeological site to be sectioned and systematically cleaned and surveyed with either sketches or photographs.

AIRLIFT TUBE
A long tube, controlled from the surface, which sucks up water, removing the sediments around the archaeological remains and cleaning the area.

Environmental Archaeology

The purpose of this branch of archaeology is to analyze the relationships between the different human societies of past times and their natural environments by studying the remains of plants and animals.

Reconstructing the Environment

Environmental archaeology has answered many questions regarding the environment's effect on the inhabitants of Earth and vice versa. Studying sediment and fossil remains enables the climate, vegetation and animals of each age and place to be determined, leading to conclusions about the eating habits and the disappearance of some civilizations, among other information. Environmental archaeology has two main branches, archaeozoology and archaeobotany, which in turn have numerous sub-disciplines.

Archaeobotany

Its purpose is to reconstruct the vegetation that existed at a specific time in the past. To achieve this, two types of remains are analyzed: macro and microbotanical. Seeds and fruit, carbonized or not, are included in the first group; the second focuses mostly on pollen, microscopic particles of which abound in sediment.

Carbonized grape. A grape from the third century BC.

Archaeozoology

This is the study of animal remains found in archaeological excavations. The analysis covers all human use of animals, whether as food, raw material for making tools and instruments, or as a workforce. In addition, knowing what the animals were like in each era also provides clues about overall environmental conditions of the time.

Horses. Skeletons found in Shandong (China).

POLLEN GRAIN
Fossilized pollen grains collected in the sediment of this lake revealed the existence of a palm forest that disappeared one thousand years ago.

Palynology

The study of fossilized pollen grains enables the vegetation from a certain place and time in the past to be reconstructed. This provides information about the climate, soil, and even the life of the inhabitants. This is possible because the outside shell of the pollen grain is very resistant and can survive for tens of thousands of years.

SEDIMENT COLUMN
It contains a myriad of plant and animal remains. Radiocarbon dating indicates the age of each stratus.

RANO KAU LAKE
An environmental archaeology study analyzed the fossilized pollen of this lake on Easter Island to determine whether there were forests there in prehistoric times, which over time would have disappeared.

Paleobotany and Paleoethnobotany

These two disciplines form the core of archaeobotany, and therefore of environmental archaeology. Paleobotany is the study of land and water plant fossils, while paleoethnobotany studies bygone interactions between humans and plants.

Alethopteris aquilinus. Fossil of a fern found in Bradwell Wood (United Kingdom).

High-Altitude Archaeology

This discipline, started in 1901 by the Swedish expedition of Erland Nordenskiöld to Mount Chañi (Argentina), has led to the finding of several Inca mummies buried in the "high sanctuaries" of the Andes, as well as other discoveries.

High Altitude Cemeteries

Burials at high altitude are another of the amazing feats of the Inca; some of them are more than 6,000 meters above sea level. The Inca reached these altitudes about 400 years before modern mountaineers, in order to perform a ritual called Capacocha (human sacrifice, usually of children) at the chosen mountaintops, which were sacred.

ORNAMENTS
A metal plate adorns the girl's head. Her face was exposed to light-ning atop Llullaillaco, after her death.

PERU

BRAZIL

▲ Ampato Volcano
(6300 m)

BOLIVIA

Llullaillaco Volcano (6739 m) ▲
Socompa Volcano (6031 m) ▲
PARAGUAY

Mount Morado ▲ (5200 m)
▲ Nevado de Chañi (5896 m)

▲ Galan Volcano (6000 m)

CHILE

ARGENTINA

FINDINGS
Most archaeological sites located in the high mountains are concen-trated among the peaks of the Andes.

▲ Mount El Plomo (5400 m)

Why So High?

There are different theories about why the Inca performed their rituals at such high points on the mountain, but the most widespread is their obsession with the worship of the Sun. In these sanctuaries, most facing toward the East, they would have felt close to the King of Stars.

The Right Temperature

The remains found at high altitudes require special conditions for preservation. The Inca mummy known as "Juanita" is displayed in a glass capsule with a constant temperature of -19°C. A modified packaged terminal air conditioner (PTAC) is used for this purpose.

"Juanita." The most famous of the Inca mummies was found atop the Ampato volcano in 1995. She had been there for more than five hundred years.

A Global Benchmark

American archaeologist and mountaineer Johan Reinhard has led the most outstanding expeditions at high altitude in recent decades. He located the mummy "Juanita" in 1995 on Mount Ampato (Peru) and three mummified children in 1999 in the Llullaillaco volcano (Argentina).

The Lightning Girl. One of the mummies found in Llullaillaco, at an altitude of 6,739 m, discovered by Johan Reinhard.

HAIR
The hair is carefully combed, and two thin braids frame her face. About twenty artifacts were found near her body.

SKIN
Despite having been struck by lightning on the shoulder, chest, and ear, the Lightning Girl's skin is remarkably well-preserved.

The Expedition to Llullaillaco

1 **Excavation**
Once the site was located, Johan Reinhard's expedition began excavating using archaeological tools and techniques. Accessing the remains proved difficult.

2 **Unearthing**
Once the three mummies were extracted, they were carefully unwrapped and provisionally protected with snow and foam rubber sheets.

3 **Descent**
Then they began the descent, with the mummies loaded on their backs. Trucks equipped with dry ice took them to their final destination in the city of Salta.

Fossil Restoration

Technology and the various techniques used in paleontology allow fossil remains of vertebrates to be successfully restored and reconstructed with great accuracy, though it is a slow and arduous task.

A Long and Delicate Process

The journey from the discovery of a fossil to the completion of its laborious restoration in a museum involves numerous stages that must be carried out with extreme care and patience. When dealing with the remains of a vertebrate, the reconstruction process can take many years and involves experts from different disciplines. Although there are many steps, two general phases are recognized: the first being cleaning and the second assembly.

Computer Analysis

Computerized tomography creates a three-dimensional image that shows the inside of the scanned object. With fossils, this enables the contents of the sample to be seen and the organic remains to be differentiated from the rock.

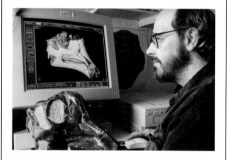

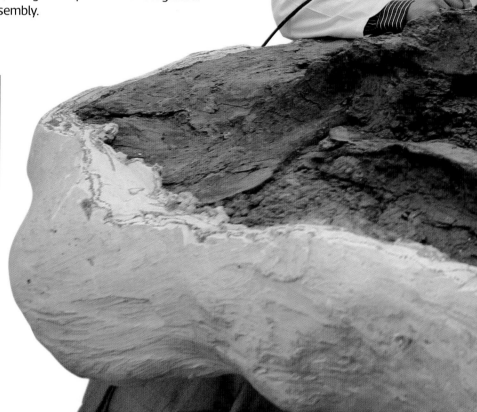

Restoration Step-by-Step

1 **Finding the Fossil**
The excavation and re-trieval of the fossil requires tools ranging from excavators and pneumatic drills to small brushes. The priority is to not damage the piece.

2 **Protection and Transfer**
Many fossils are fortified with glue to keep them together. The largest are covered in plaster before they are moved.

3 **Cleaning**
The plaster is re-moved with saws and scissors. Next, if pos-sible, the detailed form of the fossil is separated from the rock it is adhered to, and then cleaned.

Release from the Rock

In the laboratory, the fossil is separated from the rock to which it is joined. If the rock is soft, such as sandstone, applying a surfactant substance can be sufficient. If it is hard, then chisels, electric hammers, or jets of hot air may need to be used.

MOLDS FOR REPLICAS
Different materials can be used according to the type of fossil, including plaster, latex, silicone, elastic alginate, resins, and others.

SPECIFIC TOOLS
To remove the fragments most firmly adhered to the fossil, specific tools such as pneumatic chipping hammers are used.

INSTRUMENTS
Other elements for cleaning are chisels and awls of different sizes, and small circular saws.

PARENT ROCK
Some fossils, such as the impression of a plant, cannot be separated from the rock. Restoration involves refining and cleaning the rock fragment containing the fossil.

4 Casting Bones
Many fossils are far too fragile to put on display. In such cases, copies are made from molds of the original. The result is an almost exact replica.

5 Assembly
When reconstructing a skeleton, the final assembly is carried out based on scientific evidence and models created by a computer program.

Facial Reconstruction

In addition to being a valuable technology in the field of medicine, computerized tomography also has a practical application in archaeology –it allows approximate facial reconstructions to be made from cranial remains.

Advanced Technology

Computerized tomography is a diagnostic system which, instead of taking a single X-ray image (as conventional radiography does), takes several, and as a result provides a cross section of a body part. In 1972, a scanner was invented to do the job digitally and process it through a computer. In 1996, the volume generation technique was created to obtain 3D images. This technology was used in early 2005 to examine the tomb of Tutankhamen.

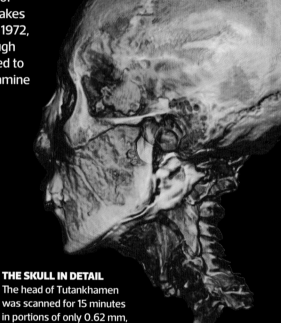

A Long-Time Aspiration

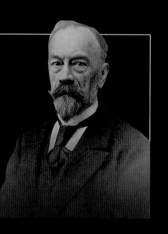

The first ones to try reconstructing a face were the forensic doctors Karl Wilhelm von Kupffer (shown in image) and Friedrich Carl Bessel-Hagen. In 1881 they made a facial replica of the philosopher Immanuel Kant, who died in 1804.

THE SKULL IN DETAIL
The head of Tutankhamen was scanned for 15 minutes in portions of only 0.62 mm, in order to show its complex structures in detail.

Other Facial Reconstructions

Jesus Christ
Forensic doctor Richard Neave and a team from the BBC reconstructed his face using a skull from the first century found in Jerusalem.

Richard III
After the discovery of the remains of this fifteenth century English king in Leicester, a tomography of the skull was taken and his face reconstructed.

Copernicus
This reconstruction was performed at the University of Warsaw with a skull found in the cathedral of Frombork (Poland).

Priestess of Chornancap
Researchers at the Utah Valley University refashioned the physiognomy of this sovereign of Lambayeque in 2012.

Teotihuacan
Two skulls of Teotihuacan inhabitants enabled scientists at the National University of Mexico to reconstruct the face of a typical inhabitant.

The Face of the King

In the case of Tutankhamen, in addition to the data collected by tomography, several sculptures of the Pharaoh and his relatives were used as a reference point. The goal was to reconstruct the appearance of the young king at the time of his death, more than 3,000 years ago.

How the Reconstruction Was Carried Out

Three teams of artists and forensic doctors from different countries participated in reconstructing the young Pharaoh's face. They worked separately and later collated the results, which turned out to be similar.

Scanning

The computerized to-mography scanner took around 1,700 digital x-ray images of the mummy, which were then fed into the computer processor.

3D Model

With the help of specific software, a volumetric projection was carried out, which enabled the deceased to be viewed as a 3D image.

Reconstruction

Based on the 3D image, forensic anthropologists worked on a skull mold and reconstructed the face of Tutankhamen (right).

SKIN COLOR
The color of Tutankhamen's skin is unknown. The restorers worked from paintings and old busts of the Pharaoh.

Infrared Photography

Archaeologists use this type of photograph to locate new underground hidden deposits or to examine ancient texts that had become unintelligible to the human eye due to wear over the centuries.

Thermal Radiation

Within the electromagnetic spectrum, the margin visible to the human eye ranges between red and violet, in a wavelength of between 700 and 400 nanometers (nm). Ultraviolet rays are a form of radiation that have a higher frequency than the color violet; on the other side, infrared rays, have a lower frequency than that of red. Infrared radiation, or thermal radiation, indicates the heat emitted by a body. There are photographic filters that allow only infrared or ultraviolet light to filter through, enabling images to be acquired that cannot be seen by the naked eye.

ELECTROMAGNETIC SPECTRUM

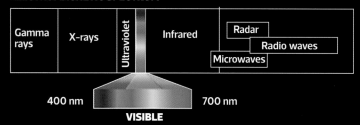

Dead Sea Scrolls

When photographing these scrolls using a camera with an infrared filter, the lens records the difference between the heat reflected by the ink and that on the parchment, offering a clear image with good contrast. This technique has made the recovery of many fragments possible.

Aerial Images

New archaeological remains have been located using aerial infrared photographs. One example is the old Roman city of Altinum, near Venice. An infrared image taken during a drought revealed the presence of a great walled city with monuments, theaters, houses, etc.

Altinum. *Science Magazine* published this digitally treated infrared image where the structure of the city can be seen.

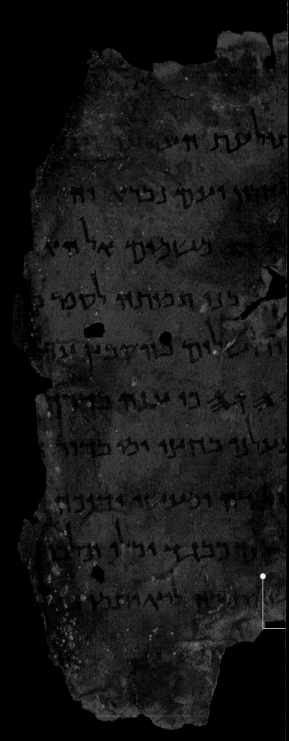

Errors of the Past

Not all techniques have been as successful as infrared photography. In the case of manuscripts, up-to-date scientists have had to clean away damaging cellulose sticky tape used by the initial researchers to hold the fragments together.

WITH INFRARED
The text can be read with greater clarity. The first photos of these manuscripts were taken during the 1950s.

WITHOUT INFRARED
The surface of the parchment has darkened over time and prevents a clear reading of the text.

Infrared Filter

In order to capture an infrared image, the camera must include a special filter that blocks ultraviolet rays and almost all of the visible spectrum. It is also necessary to use a film that is especially sensitive to wavelengths that range from 700 to 1,200 nm; those that correspond to infrared radiation.

Robot Explorers

The innumerable applications of robotics have found a place in archaeology. In recent decades, the development of small robots specifically designed for particular types of exploration has made way for important discoveries.

A New Tool for Archaeology

Small in size, and equipped with cameras, scanners, drills, and other tools depending on the case, robots allow for exploration in places that are difficult or impossible to access. They were used for the first time inside the Great Pyramid of Giza (Egypt) in 1992.

IN ACTION. A robot uses a drill to perforate the slab that closes the conduit in the lower south ventilation tunnel of the Great Pyramid.

The Upuaut Pioneers

The first robot explorer built was the Upuaut ("The opener of ways" in Arabic). It was used to explore the upper conduits of the pyramid of Khufu. Shortly afterward, an improved version was developed—the Upuaut-2 (illustration), which toured the lower ducts.

The Great Pyramid

The pyramid of Khufu in Giza has four narrow ventilation ducts. In order to explore them, a robot was designed and built especially for this task.

Upper South Conduit

Upper North Conduit

Chamber of the King

S

78.43 m

N

77.55 m

Lower South Conduit

Lower North Conduit

Entrance

Original Profile of the Pyramid

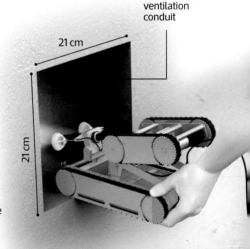

Mouth of the ventilation conduit

21 cm

21 cm

CUSTOM-MADE. The Upuaut was custom-built to carry out its mission.

The Robots of Teotihuacan

In Mexico, robots have been used to explore a tunnel that is underneath the Temple of the Feathered Serpent, at the ruins of the ancient city of Teotihuacan, founded in the second century BC. In 2013, the robot Tlaloc–II–TC managed to discover three unknown chambers using a scanner.

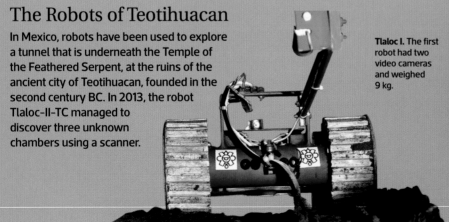

Tlaloc I. The first robot had two video cameras and weighed 9 kg.

TLALOC–II–TC: AN IMPROVED VERSION
The second robot weighed 35 kg, and featured improvements in mobility, scanning, and the addition of a robot "bug" with an infrared camera that can separate from the main vehicle.

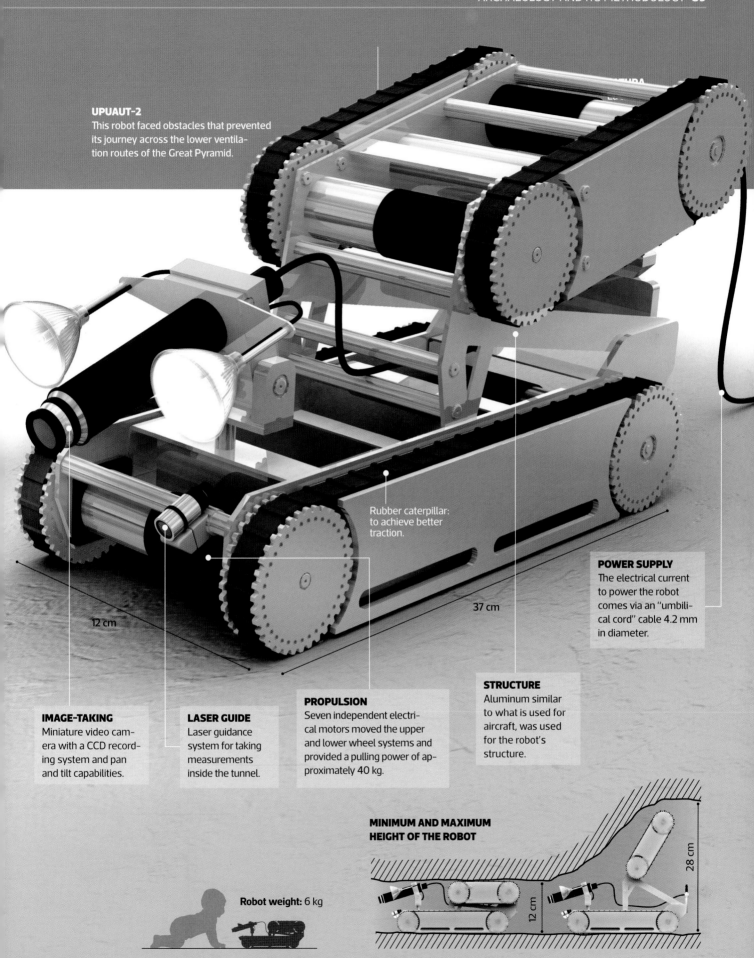

UPUAUT-2
This robot faced obstacles that prevented its journey across the lower ventilation routes of the Great Pyramid.

Rubber caterpillar: to achieve better traction.

12 cm

37 cm

POWER SUPPLY
The electrical current to power the robot comes via an "umbilical cord" cable 4.2 mm in diameter.

IMAGE-TAKING
Miniature video camera with a CCD recording system and pan and tilt capabilities.

LASER GUIDE
Laser guidance system for taking measurements inside the tunnel.

PROPULSION
Seven independent electrical motors moved the upper and lower wheel systems and provided a pulling power of approximately 40 kg.

STRUCTURE
Aluminum similar to what is used for aircraft, was used for the robot's structure.

Robot weight: 6 kg

MINIMUM AND MAXIMUM HEIGHT OF THE ROBOT

28 cm

12 cm

Identifying Mummies

Establishing the identity of a person who died thousands of years ago requires a multidisciplinary process in which information from historical texts are combined with archaeological findings, anthropological information, and technological advances in medicine.

Technology: A Strong Ally

Computerized Axial Tomography (CAT) makes the study of mummified bodies possible without invasive practices. DNA identification tests and X-rays are also invaluable for confirming a person's identity.

DNA Analysis

DNA identification tests have revolutionized the world of Egyptology. Thanks to this technology, mummies such as Akhenaten and Queen Tiye (his mother), have been identified. Kinship relations have also been confirmed, as has the practice of royal incest during the Eighteenth Dynasty.

1 Free from Contamination
After selecting the mummy to be researched, geneticists take the necessary protective measures to avoid contaminating it with traces of their own DNA.

2 Selection of Sample
Samples are taken from the tissue of different parts of the mummy, preferably from inside the bones, the area most protected from outer contamination.

3 Analysis
The genetic composition is analyzed in the laboratory. After isolating the chromosomes, the gender is established and the markers and alleles are located within the genetic sequences.

4 Matches
To confirm kinships, the alleles are compared with those from possible relatives. If there are matches in at least eight of these segments, the paternal or maternal relationship is confirmed.

Tomography

This imaging system, which provides three-dimensional, high-resolution images, can detect anomalies with great accuracy. This facilitates the identification of the deceased by contrasting the result of the scan with biographical data.

MUMMY TAHEMAA
In 2009, a team of British radiologists scanned this mummy that is over more than 2,500 years old. It is known that Tahemaa lived in Luxor and passed away at the age of 28.

DISCOVERY
The tomographic analysis of Tahemaa unveiled something unusual: the brain was left in the mummy. This indicates the possibility that she was embalmed by an apprentice.

Documentary Support

The existing lists of Ancient Egyptian kings are essential references for identifying mummies. The Aegyptiaka of the Priest Manetho (second century BC), a work featuring biographies of the great Pharaohs, also contributes significant information for connecting the mummies with the well-known sovereigns.

ROYAL LISTS
Those found at Karnak, Abydos (in image), and Saqqara, along with the Stone of Palermo and the Turin King List, contain key information.

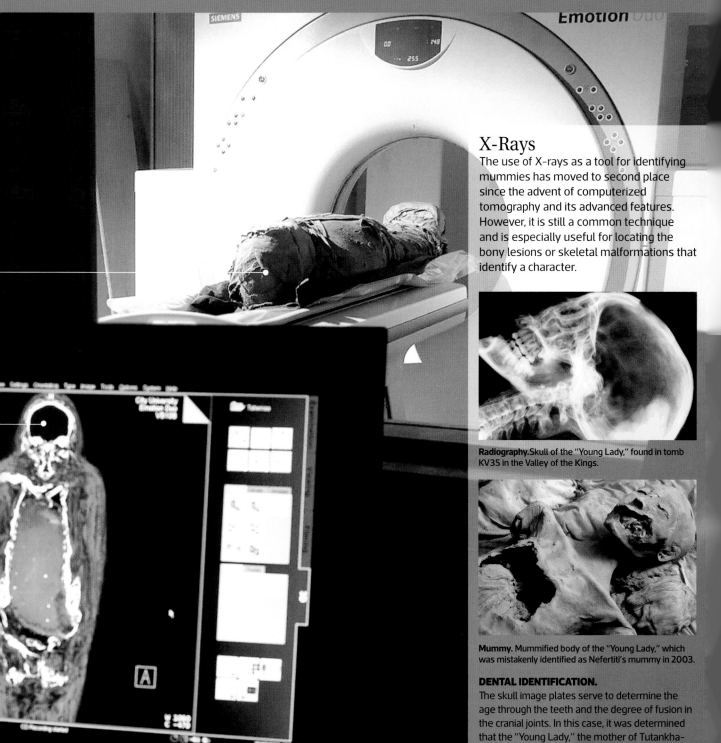

X-Rays

The use of X-rays as a tool for identifying mummies has moved to second place since the advent of computerized tomography and its advanced features. However, it is still a common technique and is especially useful for locating the bony lesions or skeletal malformations that identify a character.

Radiography. Skull of the "Young Lady," found in tomb KV35 in the Valley of the Kings.

Mummy. Mummified body of the "Young Lady," which was mistakenly identified as Nefertiti's mummy in 2003.

DENTAL IDENTIFICATION.
The skull image plates serve to determine the age through the teeth and the degree of fusion in the cranial joints. In this case, it was determined that the "Young Lady," the mother of Tutankhamun, was about 25 when she died.

AMPHITHEATER A building, usually round or oval, with a central space for the presentation of dramatic or sporting events.

ANTECHAMBER A small room that leads to a main one.

ANTHROPOMORPHISM The giving of human characteristics to a god, animal, or object.

AZIMUTH The direction of a celestial object from the observer, expressed as the angular distance from the north or south point of the horizon to the point at which a vertical circle passing through the object intersects the horizon.

BIPEDAL Describing an animal that uses only two legs for walking.

DENOTE A sinkhole that results from the collapse of limestone bedrock that exposes the water underneath.

FRIEZE A broad horizontal band of sculpted or painted decoration, especially on a wall near the ceiling.

GLYPH A pictographic character or symbol.

HIEROGLYPH A stylized picture of an object representing a word, syllable, or sound.

HOMINOID A primate of a group that includes humans, their fossil ancestors, and the great apes.

HYPOTHESIS An explanation made on the basis of limited evidence.

IDEOGRAM A written character symbolizing the idea of a thing without indicating the sounds used to say it.

METHODOLOGY A system used in a particular area of study or activity.

NECROPOLIS A large cemetery belonging to an ancient city.

NEOLITHIC Relating to the later part of the Stone Age.

OBSIDIAN Dark, smooth volcanic rock formed by the rapid solidification of lava without crystallization.

PALEOLITHIC Relating to the early phase of the Stone Age.

PAPYRI A material prepared in ancient Egypt for writing or painting on and also for making rope, sandals, and boats.

PHONOGRAM A symbol representing a sound.

POLYCHROME Describing something that is painted or decorated in several colors.

SIMIAN Resembling apes or monkeys.

STRATUM A layer of rock in the ground.

SURFACTANT A substance that tends to reduce the surface tension of a liquid in which it is dissolved.

TERRACOTTA Unglazed earthenware used as ornamental building material or in modeling.

TOMOGRAPHY A technique for using X-rays or ultrasound to display a cross section of a human body or other solid object.

American Anthropological Association

2300 Clarendon Blvd., Suite 1301

Arlington, VA 22201

(703) 528-1902

Website: www.americananthro.org

Founded in 1902 and based in Washington, DC, the American Anthropological Association is the world's largest association for professional anthropologists.

Archaeological Institute of America Headquarters (AIA)

Located at Boston University

656 Beacon Street, 6th Floor

Boston, MA 02215-2006 USA

(617) 353-9361

Website: www.archaeological.org

The Archaeological Institute of America (AIA) is a not-for-profit group founded in 1879. It is North America's oldest and largest organization devoted to the world of archaeology.

Canadian Archaeological Association

Indigenous Studies and History

Brantford Campus

Wilfrid Laurier University

73 George St.

Brantford, ON N3T 2Y3

Canada

Website: www.canadianarchaeology.com

Founded in 1968, the Canadian Archaeological Association (CAA) invites professional, avocational, and student archaeologists.

Society for Historical Archaeology

13017 Wisteria Drive #395

Germantown, MD 20874

(301) 972-9684

Website: www.sha.org

Formed in 1967, the Society for Historical Archaeology (SHA) is the largest scholarly group concerned with the archaeology of the modern world (A.D. 1400–present) and promotes scholarly research and the dissemination of knowledge concerning historical archaeology.

Websites

Because of the changing nature of internet links, Rosen Publishing has developed an online list of websites related to the subject of this book. This site is updated regularly. Please use this link to access the list:

http://www.rosenlinks.com/VHW/archaeology

Beard, Mary. *The Fires of Vesuvius : Pompeii Lost and Found.* Cambridge, MA: Harvard University Press, 2008.

Brier, Bob. *The Secret Of The Great Pyramid: How One Man's Obsession Led To The Solution Of Ancient Egypt's Greatest Mystery.* Washington, DC: Smithsonian Books, 2008.

Carlsen, William. *Jungle Of Stone: The True Story Of Two Men, Their Extraordinary Journey, And The Discovery Of The Lost Civilization Of The Maya.* New York, NY: William Morrow, 2016.

Catling, Christopher. *A Practical Handbook Of Archaeology: A Beginner's Guide To Unearthing The Past.* London, England: Hermes House, 2014.

Connelly, Joan B. *The Parthenon Enigma.* New York, NY: Alfred A. Knopf, 2014.

Down, David. *The Archaeology Book.* Green Forest, AR: Master Books, 2010.

Hunt, Terry L., and Carl P. Lipo. *The Statues That Walked: Unraveling The Mystery Of Easter Island.* Berkeley, CA: Counter Point Press, 2012.

Pearson, Michael. *Stonehenge : A New Understanding: Solving The Mysteries Of The Greatest Stone Age Monument.* New York, NY: The Experiment, 2013.

Ray, J. D. *Rosetta Stone And The Rebirth Of Ancient Egypt.* Cambridge, MA: Harvard University Press, 2012.

Tyldesley, Joyce A. *Tutankhamen: The Search For An Egyptian King.* New York, NY: Basic Books, 2012.

For Further Reading

Index